The Pocket Guide For

SALES
SURVIVAL

To: _____

From: _____

I am giving this book to you because these are the sales essentials…
This is your Guide For Survival.

Personal Note: _____

_____
_____
_____
_____
_____
_____
_____
_____
_____

Island of Sales

Copyright

THE POCKET GUIDE FOR SALES SURVIVAL

"5 Thumbs Up! After reading this incredible book you will know how to sell me three additional thumbs."
– Erik Qualman, #1 Best Selling Author of Socialnomics and Digital Leader

"A truly inspirational book! Very fun and packed with tons of great practical tips for sales professionals at any level. Highly recommended!"
– Dr. Edward Hult – CEO, EF North America

"The Pocket Guide For Sales Survival is such a practical book, filled with so much useful knowledge about sales that I think it should be in the hands of any person pursuing a career in sales, business or Entrepreneurship of any kind."
– Desh Deshpande, Co-Chairman of the National Advisory Council on Innovation and Entrepreneurship.

"I thought the concept and content of the book were both terrific! I will be purchasing copies for my entire sales force, as I think it is just the sort of easy read and common sense approach that they need!"
– Mark Santschi, Division Manager, Advanced Pneumatics Company and APC Automation

"The Pocket Guide For Sales Survival" has value for both entry level and veteran sales professionals. I feel a long term relationship developing with this concise and clever sales guide. Jason and Randy believe a sales career should be both fun and challenging, with the emphasis on fun!"
– Howard Rubenstein – President and Principal – Rubenstein Careers

Testimonials

"As an experienced recruiter who places sales and digital marketing professionals, I found there to be an endless amount of great information in 'The Pocket guide For Sales Survival' that will help job seekers not only in their search, but also to become more effective salespeople once they start their new job."

– Scott White, Search Director, HireMindsLLC

"Whether you are a recent graduate entering sales or a seasoned professional, The Pocket Guide For Sales survival offers knowledgeable tips and reminders of how to succeed for your organization and for yourself. This book is a recommended read for sales professionals of all levels. I will definitely be encouraging my sales students to have a copy on their desk."

– Dr. Michael Rodriguez, PhD. Chandler Family Sales Center - Elon University

"As the owner and CEO of a company that employs mostly salespeople, I understand the importance of solid reference material to keep your sales team focused, inspired and prepared. This book allows us to deliver the perfect lesson at the right moment. In short - it allows my team to be more successful. This is a great book if you are new to sales or have been selling for years. The book's price is an investment in your future profits."

– Mark Eldridge - CEO – Salestart

"I am fascinated with the timeless wisdom that is loaded into this book. Brand new salespeople will find great tips, and veterans will find subtle keepsakes to the simplicity of closing deals. This is undoubtedly one of the greatest collections of vital sales knowledge I have ever come across. A must have for anyone passionate about winning, closing deals, and fine tuning habits that lead to success."
—Jaime Hepp- Business Owner, Consultant, Board Member at Boys & Girls Club of Venice

"I regularly reference this book, The Pocket Guide For Sales Survival, to stay sharp. It's the first book I've read since "How to Win Friends and Influence People" that I feel should be required reading for anyone interested in sales—every student or teacher of sales, every salesperson new or experienced, every sales manager and director. It is an indispensable part of my library that I constantly revisit."
—Joe Harvey - Sales Trainer - EF Education First

"This isn't something applicable to just one industry. I reference these tips with our internal sales team at an international development consulting firm (2,300 people in 70 countries, Abt Associates) and I've also built them into the sales model for a medical device startup. A big part of creating the right culture in a company is giving them a common language to communicate. In software development it might be ITIL or Agile/SCRUM. In project management it's the PMP or CMMI. For sales, it's this book. There is this creative, exponential energy when the team is strategizing new client acquisition, using the world's best practices as their starting point!"
— Jeff Takle - Director of the Innovation Lab - Abt Associates

About the Author
JASON DEAMATO

I had no idea I was working in sales when I first started selling orthopedic supplies back in 1998.

All I was told was "go around to these doctor's offices, be yourself and build relationships, show them the stuff, if they seem interested get their information and I'll take it from there."

If you had asked me what I did back then I would have said "I work with orthopedic and post-surgical equipment but I also play guitar in a band" or something like that. I would have tried to sound important and cool and mentioning *sales* didn't seem to accomplish either.

Now if someone asks me what I do, I proudly say "I'm in sales"

I consider myself extremely lucky to say that. I found my calling in sales and I love everything about it. And even more than selling I adore breaking down the process, teaching, and hopefully motivating, and inspiring salespeople to be the absolute best they can be. But first and foremost educating people on what being in "sales" really is, breaking down the stigmas that have existed for close to a century.

When I see heads nodding in a crowd, I am at my happiest. As long as I get to continue this journey I will be eternally grateful.

After years of experience, and failing a million times at a million different things I am happy to share those experiences to help people succeed. I am grateful for every failure and success, and when it comes down to it, I just love "talking sales." Almost as much as I love talking music.

Unfortunately nobody pays me to talk about music, so until that day comes. Sales it is.

About the Author
RANDY BERNARD

I was born and raised just north of Boston and followed in my parent's footsteps into sales. After building my career mainly on the west coast, I settled back in Massachusetts with my wife Jamie-Lynn and our hilarious children. I currently run sales for a great software company in Boston.

While much has changed in the world around me during my career, there is one thing that has never changed; the existence of a quota. I am as familiar with having a quota as I am with breathing. I have had a monthly quota for every-single-month of my life for 20 straight years.

Everyone knows the stresses associated with a career, marriage or parenting but how about also having a "must-hit" quota that resets every 30 days for 240 months in a row?!?! It adds up to a lot of pressure, especially when you take quotas very seriously, like I do.

Underneath the challenge of straight quota for two decades, I've accumulated some remarkable stories, uncovered many mistakes and learned valuable lessons which I look forward to sharing with you.

Having held every role in sales from the entry level to the VP, I believe that my hands on experience is my greatest asset with which to help other salespeople hit their goals.

A positive attitude and a killer work ethic can get you very far, but to be top of your class in sales it takes additional skills. I enjoy teaching those skills through sales training, motivational speaking and consulting and have fallen in love with helping people learn the art of selling.

Teaching someone how to increase their closing percentage, rebound from a slump or crush their number is what I love to do more than anything!

Enjoy the book, Randy B.

The Authors

The Pocket Guide For

SALES
SURVIVAL

Introduction

WE LIVE ON THE ISLAND OF SALES.

Salespeople are different. We don't follow the same career paths that other people do. True salespeople live someplace different. We live on an island … "The Island of Sales." Yes, as salespeople, we love to think of ourselves as living on "The Island of Sales."

We want to encourage every reader to think this way too.

The sooner salespeople become proud of working in sales, the sooner they will hone the precise skills needed to find record-breaking success.

You should be very proud to represent some of the hardest working people in the world.

Sales projections and results dictate almost every decision made in business. What we do is just too important not to be proud.

If you work in sales, no matter what your title, you will never feel like you have enough hours in your day. Salesperson, Vice President, Director, or Manager—it doesn't matter. If you work in sales, you know this feeling all too well.

Often, there is little time to train (or to be trained) on the hundreds of behaviors salespeople must practice in their careers. We were lucky to have mentors who imparted this wisdom to us despite having demanding careers.

This is our way of spreading what we learned into an easy to read guide.

The Pocket Guide For Sales Survival

The goal of this book is quite simple: to compile a list of indispensable sales rules that is not only a quick read, but also serves as a fun daily reference for anyone working in sales. This book was inspired by many of the great books that influence and empower people. It was also inspired by many of the books that take up countless valuable hours to read, with only two or three golden nuggets of information buried deep within the pages.

This is a simple reference guide that can—and should—be used daily and is very easy to open and be learning right away. Nothing is buried deep; it is all a page flip away.

Our goal is to be as SUCCINCT as we possibly can.

This book is divided into 4 simple buckets that reflect the different stages that make up the path of a salesperson's career.

Beginner – Arriving to the Island
Intermediate – Checking Into Your Villa
Advanced – Extended Island Vacationer
Expert – Island Resident
You can read this book in one night and then reference it every day for the rest of your career.

If you want to get the most out of this book and see results, keep it nearby at all times.

In a world ruled by social media, with 140-character tweets, Facebook updates and ever-changing mobile technology, who has time to read every 350-page sales book out there?

I often contemplate the multitude of rules that salespeople need to keep fresh in their heads. Quite frankly, it's overwhelming. There is so much to remember.

The key to becoming a great salesperson is to practice certain behaviors until they become second-nature habits. Just as the key to becoming a great golfer is usually private lessons, driving range, and playing many rounds until your technique and muscle memory is second nature.

That is what this book is meant to be: a resource a salesperson can flip through daily to **teach and remind** them of the techniques and theories that they should be working on—and using.

The rules of a successful sales career are in your hands.

Sales Culture

Not only do we want to keep the rules brief and to the point, but we also tried to keep them entertaining.

Instead of a manager pulling a salesperson into a meeting to discuss their lack of enthusiasm, the manager can instead shoot their salesperson an email that reads, "Rule #16 Brian ... Rule #16."

Brian grabs his Pocket Guide For Sales Survival and sees "Rule #16: Be Enthusiastic." Got it! A quick and effective way to communicate when the situation dictates such.

When salespeople adopt positive behaviors, it spreads and leads to a successful culture. If people are yelling across your sales floor, "Rule #16!"

Introduction

you know you have an intelligent sales floor that understands the true value of the universal sales laws.

Which rules will be your favorites?
Which rules do you already execute well?
Which rules do you need to work on?
Let the fun begin!

It All Starts with Your Thinking

It would be quite daunting to try and execute every rule in this book on a daily basis, but if you skim through the rules every morning walking to your office, or keep this book on your desk for frequent browsing, you will be recharging your brain with the knowledge and reminders you need to be successful. Converting rules on a page into behaviors in your daily routine is how you become elite.

If you want to get better at sales, you first have to decide to take action. Once the way you think has changed, your behavior can follow. Everything starts with your thoughts and ends with your results.

Thoughts > Feelings > Behavior > Results

The Bottom Line

We hope you enjoy the brevity and flow of this book. Just as quickly as you digest one rule you can move on to the next.

Read 10 rules in 10 minutes as refreshers or read one rule; and name that rule your theme for the day.

Every rule can be applicable to winning sales in certain situations.

Island Lore

At the end of each rule you will find something extra waiting for you—
"Island Lore."

We can't disclose anything additional about Island Lore at this time.

Thank You

Thank you for choosing a career path that takes commitment, instinct,
attitude and other all-too-rare attributes. You walk among the world's
elite business people.

I believe in great sales, I believe in great communication and of course I
believe in great people.

Finally, thank you for coming to The Island of Sales and giving us the
chance to share the sales rules that we know can help you on your journey to success. Having them compiled in one resource like this, gives you
an edge.

There is no better investment than investing in YOU. Remain focused
and dedicated and great things will happen.

-Jason DeAmato

Beginner

ARRIVING TO THE ISLAND

Rule 1
BE PROUD

Are you proud to be a salesperson? Stop and think about that for a minute.

Are you truly proud to call yourself a salesperson? When friends, family or even strangers ask what you do for a living, how do you respond? It's not uncommon for some salespeople to feel hesitant about admitting their line of work. Kind of like a mortician, or a Senator.

If you ever feel this way, even a little, the first rule of sales to remember is that there's nothing to be ashamed of—and everything to be proud of.

If you want to not only survive, but thrive, on The Island of Sales, you have to be proud to call it your home.

It's no surprise that some people feel ashamed to call themselves salespeople. The world is inundated with incompetent salespeople who give the entire profession a bad name. Honest salespeople, the ones who truly care about the customer and never take sneaky or lazy approaches to closing a deal, are the ones most coveted by their companies.

ISLAND LORE

How proud are we of our profession? Well, we're building an island just for salespeople! No shame there!

Working in sales is one of the most challenging—and rewarding— careers imaginable. There are 1,001 reasons why we love sales and are truly proud to call ourselves salespeople. If you want to break records and become a top salesperson, you need to be proud.

Rule 2
ATTITUDE IS EVERYTHING

We once worked with a salesman named Pete. Not only was he a top performer, but he helped build our company from the ground up. Very impressive guy.

In the beginning, Pete was great to work with. Always ready to take on a challenge, never getting too discouraged when things didn't go his way.

Then Pete got sour.

Suddenly Pete's attitude took a complete 180. To make matters worse, it soon began to spread to his colleagues in the sales department. It was starting to hurt Pete's sales—and theirs.

We had to fire Pete, our top salesperson, because he lost his positive attitude. If the sales floor was a human body, Pete's bad attitude was a cancer. We had to go in and remove the cancer before it could spread.

Having a great attitude is a requirement in sales.

It is non-negotiable and absolutely mandatory.

Why? Because you have to be able to roll with the punches, day in and day out.

You can master every other rule in this book, but without an incredibly positive attitude you will struggle just to survive in sales, let alone achieve true success.

Rule No. 2

Your attitude not only affects the person sitting next to you, but it affects relationships with your customers, your boss and your co-workers.

And of course, most important of all, it affects the people you love outside of work.

A great attitude is the key to a great life.

ISLAND LORE

If there is one thing we KNOW we have, it's great attitudes. And it's the one thing we're NEVER going to lose.

Rule 3
WORK ETHIC

Sales is a numbers game. Always has been, always will be. And since it's a numbers game, those who work the hardest WIN. Simple as that!

You can either PLAY NOW and PAY LATER or PAY NOW and PLAY LATER.

Either way you will pay.

Take it from a couple of middle aged bozos who played too much in the beginning. We wish we were playing more now!

It isn't just the fact that you will reach more people and therefore close more deals. The harder you work the more you learn what NOT to do. So the harder you work the faster you learn how to work smart!

Please don't let the brevity of this entry fool you into thinking it's any less important than the others. We just don't want you to over think it.

The Rule speaks for itself.

Work harder than everyone else.

ISLAND LORE

"Today I will do what others won't, so tomorrow I can accomplish what others can't"
– Jerry Rice

Rule No. 3

Rule 4

BELIEVE IN YOURSELF

If you don't believe in yourself, who will?

Sometimes, when you feel like you're hitting a wall or if things go wrong, you have to dig deep and really believe in yourself.

It doesn't matter if other people don't believe in you. It doesn't matter how many times you've failed. YOU have to believe in yourself—no matter what.

If you give up on yourself, so will everyone else. And never compare yourself to other people. Your life is about you and you control how much belief you have. What other people think about you…is none of your business.

Be confident, find your strengths, leverage them, and believe until the last second.

ISLAND LORE

Believe, baby! Everyone is allowed to get a little lost, but you have to take control of the situation. Otherwise, the situation will control you. The Island believes in you!

Not everyone is going to believe in you. So make sure you believe in you.

Rule 5
READY...SET...GOALS!

What do you want?

It's a broad question, we know, but it's one you have to constantly be asking yourself.

Whatever answer you come up with, whether it is a successful career, a promotion, a big sale or some chocolate ice cream, this is your goal.

And you have to set goals. Simple as that.

Setting goals is a science. Learn the different ways to set goals. There are countless goal-setting methods and ways to measure them, but the bottom line is that you have to set them. Here are a few keys to setting your goals:
• Know exactly what you want
• Be passionate about getting it
• Have a solid game plan to get there

This is the difference between dreams and truly achievable goals!

Goals keep people in check and should be set daily. There are two types of goals: action goals and result goals. Action goals are just as important, if not more important, than result goals. Make sure to always set action goals and hold yourself accountable.

Rule No. 5

More goal setting tips:
- Write goals down in a place you cannot avoid
- Have an accountability partner
- Make sure goals have a deadline
- Revise your goals if they were not realistically set
- Make sure your goals are attainable.
- If nature gets in the way (say the power goes out in your town for a few days), then revise them. But only if nature gets in the way.

ISLAND LORE

One of our goals for The Island of Sales was simple: Implement a down-to-earth approach to teaching sales, without any fancy gimmicks. Simple. Smart. Effective.

Rule 6
BE COMPETITIVE

Think about someone you know, someone who consistently achieves better results than you do. It could be a co-worker, a competitor, even a friend.

Write their name here: _____

Now go beat them. (Not with your fists! Just at something competitive!) Once you have done that, come back to this page, cross their name out and write another name here:

_____ and go beat THEM!

Those who are truly competitive ALWAYS find a way.

If you do not have an innate, burning competitive drive, force yourself to engage in some friendly competition first. You may tap into some feelings that teach you how to be more competitive.

> ## ISLAND LORE
>
> ———
>
> Jerry McGuire said it best: "You COMPETE me."
>
> That is what he said, right?

Goals, self-accountability, and competitiveness...they all mix together to form a very combustible gas. You need to douse your daily actions in that gas and light the fuse!

It's a complete game-changer.

Rule No. 6

Rule 7

LISTEN, LISTEN, LISTEN

To quote one of our favorites movies: "You shut your mouth when you're talking to me."

In a perfect sales situation, you will only do 20% of the talking, leaving the remaining 80% for the customer. You were given two ears and only one mouth for a reason.

Listening is crucial to defining needs, building relationships and being able to provide solutions. Conversely, talking a lot tends to make you sound desperate. You can lose sales that way.

ISLAND LORE

The Island is filled with people who love to listen. You will leave feeling like you just sat through therapy (without the bill, of course!)

There are two types of listening you should focus on:

• Active—you are paying attention, taking notes, remembering what is being said and verifying it back to the customer.

• Instinctive—you are listening to tone and what is BEHIND the words. You can say the same thing a million different ways, with a million different meanings. Make sure you are instinctively listening to everything behind the words.

Rule 8

HAVE INTEGRITY

Do the right thing, ESPECIALLY when nobody is watching.

Integrity is defined as the quality of being honest and having strong moral principles; moral uprightness is an essential character trait, not just in sales, but in life.

You will be challenged. There will be times in your career where it will be easier to look the other way, to take the easy route, but making the wrong choice will compromise your integrity.

In the end, this will always come back to haunt you.

Your customers deserve it (to be treated with integrity), your employer deserves it, and your employees deserve it. Everyone deserves it.

To quote Coach Taylor from Friday Night Lights, "Clear eyes, full hearts...can't lose!"

ISLAND LORE

Help us squash all the negative stereotypes that exist in sales. If you don't want to, the next ferry home leaves in 20 minutes.

Trust what your eyes are telling you when you are seeing clearly, keep your heart full and follow it. Clear eyes and a full heart will strengthen your inner integrity and guide you in the right direction.

Thank you Coach Taylor and gang!

Rule No. 8

Rule 9
CONNECT FIRST

One of the most important things to remember in sales is that first impressions are crucial and connecting with a customer will always bode well for your sales numbers.

We are not telling you to become best friends and go on vacation with someone prior to selling to them, but building a relationship, even a little casual banter for two minutes before the selling begins, is vital.

People love to talk, so ask them open-ended questions, and let them discuss anything and everything. Sooner or later it will be time to sell. Until then, don't.

Are you excited to talk about your product or service?

Are you genuinely interested in your customer's needs?

The answer should be YES!

But don't move so quickly that you forget to spend the appropriate time building a connection first.

ISLAND LORE

"People don't care how much you know until they know how much you care."
– John Maxwell

Once you establish a connection it makes the entire process much more enjoyable for everyone!

You will have plenty of time to talk about your product or service. First build that connection and then turn it into a relationship.

Rule No. 9

Rule 10

LOVE WHAT YOU DO

Have fun and enjoy what you are doing. If you can't enjoy your career, then stop and find something else.

There will be growing pains along the way to becoming a master salesperson, but if you do not LOVE what you do, something has to change.

When you love what you do, you don't work another day in your life.

There are so many opportunities that exist, keep searching until you find true happiness. Then and only then will you reach your full potential.

It's never too late to make a change.

ISLAND LORE

There's another book (besides this one) that we think is a must-read for every salesperson. If you can't find a way to love what you do after reading it … yikes, we feel bad for you! It's called "Fish" and it's written by Stephen C. Lundin, Ph.D., Harry Paul and John Christensen.

Rule No. 10

Rule 11

BE GENUINE

People can sense if you are genuine or if you are full of what makes the grass grow green.

Be genuine in every aspect of your business life.

Those who show their genuine colors tend to become the most successful—especially if those colors are appealing.

The first step is to become comfortable with yourself. If you need to work on that, you should.

True business relationships and personal relationships work best when people accept and like each other's true identity.

ISLAND LORE

It's OK to show your faults. We would rather deal with a genuine person who is confident than someone who tries to mask their weaknesses with false bravado. Show your true colors. In the end, genuine behavior always brings true happiness and results!

Of course we all have little things about us that may not be the most flattering. If you like to clear your throat like a giraffe with bronchitis, we suggest you do so, on THE WAY to the office.

Rule 12

LISTEN TO YOURSELF

The following is a step-by-step guide on how to observe your own sales calls.

You should study this process carefully, committing it to memory so you don't miss any of the complex principles or subtle nuances.

Ready? Here it is:

• Record yourself selling
• Listen to (or watch) that recording
• Fix what sucks

ISLAND LORE

We like to joke on the Island, but this is no joke. Fix what sucks! Don't make the mistake of thinking you can't improve.

Rule No. 12

Rule 13
QUALIFY YOUR CUSTOMER

Are you speaking with the decision-maker?

The evaluator?

The champion?

The end user?

The guy who waters the plants?

Qualify by asking questions and being direct:

"Now that you know about us, help me understand what happens next on your end?"

"How does your decision making process work?"

Figure it out and you will save yourself, and your prospects, a lot of time.

Over time you should get the "feel" for the whales, the bails, and the snails.

ISLAND LORE

You're not qualified to live on the Island until you've read this book. Only then will you be ready, young Skywalker. That's a Star Wars reference for all you millennials. Boy do we feel old.

Whales are great. Snails are slow and most people like to bail. If you can't feel this you better make sure your questioning is consistent!

Rule 14

MAKE THEM LAUGH

OK, not everyone was born with the gift of comedy.

We know this because we've spent our entire lives trying to make people laugh.

Results?

We hear crickets 75% of the time.

This doesn't dissuade us from trying, however. In front of prospects, being funny (or at least trying to be funny) can really break the ice and get you a lot further.

If you feel a laugh is a lock, go for it. If you have natural comedic talent, use your humor to make people feel good.

Business is serious, but you can be serious and have fun at the same time.

If you can make people laugh, you are definitely going to be remembered more than the next person. Even if all you have is a little self-deprecating humor, use it. It helps you seem more relatable and human.

GRAIN OF SAND:

The highest paid career in the U.S. is sales, even exceeding law and medicine!

Rule 15

EYE CONTACT AND A HANDSHAKE

Look people right in the eye when you communicate with them and greet them with a solid handshake. That can say a lot more about you and your product than you could ever put into words.

If you're unsure whether or not you have a good handshake, then you probably don't. So work on it.

The sale is usually made in the first 30 seconds. Don't blow it by staring at the prospect's shoes and giving them a wet noodle of a handshake.

ISLAND LORE

If your hands are constantly sweaty, consider giving hugs a try.

On the flip side, don't break someone's hand. Not many big sales deals are closed on the way to the emergency room. The waiting room, maybe…

Rule 16
BE ENTHUSIASTIC

A sale is more than just a monetary transaction. It's the transfer of enthusiasm from one person to another.

It's the toy store owner overflowing with joy as he shows the child how to drive the train under the bridge, or the travel agent exuberantly describing the soft sand and warm breeze to the retired couple considering a tropical cruise.

Enthusiasm is VERY contagious! But you can't transfer something that you don't have. Think about that.

ISLAND LORE

Your enthusiasm should always be one notch higher than your prospect's

Great enthusiasm can make up for not only a lack of confidence, but also experience and knowledge.

It can help a veterans salesperson who's losing their luster to get their swagger back.

Many sales people become less enthusiastic after selling the same thing for years. Do not fall into this trap. Your customer deserves better. Try to find something in particular that you connect with about what it is you are selling and revive your enthusiasm for it.

Rekindle that passion you once had.

As Cosmo Kramer so eloquently put it… "Well, you know what they say, you don't sell the steak, you sell the sizzle!"

Good work today K-man!

Rule No. 16

Rule 17
USE THEIR NAME

Everyone loves to hear their own name. When you address someone by their name, it not only personalizes your conversation, it shows you are paying close attention to them.

When you use your customer's name, you will keep their attention.

Don't overdo it though. There's a simple solution:

"The Three Time Rule."

Use the customer's name once at the beginning of your pitch, once in the middle and, yes, once when you say goodbye.

Quick Tip: Unless it's obvious, you might want to be sure you are pronouncing their name correctly first, if it's something they are going to hear you repeat three times.

ISLAND LORE

We'd like to take a moment to personally thank everyone who's bought this book so far. Thank you, Aaron ... Abe ... Ace ... Adam ... Albert ... Andrea ... Andy ... Bart ... Beth ... Becky... Burt...Caleb...Chris...

Rule 18

BE POLITE

Use profanity, pick your nose, be loud, antagonize, tell offensive jokes, chew with your mouth open, show up late, criticize everything, constantly interrupt the prospect and always use the following line:

"Either you sign now, or I'm walking out of here because I don't need to waste my time on an idiot who doesn't understand the value in my product."

ISLAND LORE

As you (hopefully) realized, that is a list of things you SHOULDN'T do while selling. In reality, please be polite. Thank you. The world needs more politeness!

Rule 19
SMILE

Wake up on the wrong side of the bed?

Saddened by something horrible in the news?

Run out of gas on the highway?

Smile. Like a lot of things in life…
it's free!

When it comes to selling…

Lose a deal at the last minute?

New leads are not quite what you
expected?

Just missed bonus this month?
Smile….

ISLAND LORE

It's hard not to smile on
the Island. The sun is
always shining, the sand
is always soft, the water
is always blue and the
inhabitants are always
closing.

It's guaranteed to make you, and your prospect, happier.

When you're meeting someone in person, be personable, warm and
friendly.

Even when you're on the phone, don't forget to smile. You better believe
your prospect will be able to hear the difference.

Smile and dial, baby!

Rule 20

SPREAD GOOD VIBES

If you do things that make other people feel good, it makes you feel good. What a concept!

Set a goal to do three things every day to help others and spread your positivity.

Heck, even one random act of kindness a day is enough.

Life is short. Do good.

ISLAND LORE

The Island is all about good vibes … it's an island!

"Let's get together and feel alright"

– Bob Marley

Rule 21

SLOW DOWN

In sales, talkingtoofastisadeathwish.

If you're a fast talker, you need to change your ways. You need to ... slow ... yourself ... down.

Remember, people only retain about 10% of what you say anyway, so don't make it any harder for them to grasp your points.

Also remember they NEED to remember it. And they may be hearing it for the first time!

Slow down. Check in.

You want to talk ... "at a medium pace."

Although you have always talked fast, with enough practice you can break this habit.

Rule 22

DON'T BE DESPERATE

Is there anything more desperate than a guy who hasn't been on a date in years? Poor guy.

But the thing is, that "poor guy" is going to remain "poor" until he loses the desperate vibe.

Just like in the dating world, customers can sense desperation in a salesperson.

And it's a major turnoff.

> ## ISLAND LORE
>
> ———
>
> Desperation leads to separation—separation from you and everything you want.

Keep your chin up, brother (and sister, too). Change your online dating status from "Lonely but Nice" to "Ready to Rock."

All is fair in love and sales.

None of your customers are having this conversation "Mary seemed more desperate than any other salesperson I've come across. Let's give her the business. I think she needs that commission!"

Rule 23
NEVER COMPLAIN

Have a headache? Go take some aspirin.

Complaining never helps and only hurts. Only share negatives with people who can help solve your problems.

Be a problem-solver, not a problem-finder. If you identify an obstacle or a problem, try to provide some solutions.

Unless you're asking your colleague for an aspirin, complaining to them about your splitting headache only creates more headaches. Simple rule of thumb:

ISLAND LORE

There's no complaining on the Island. First of all, it's annoying, and second of all, it is really annoying.

At work, if you have a problem, you can share it with a superior or a subordinate. Not a peer.

Only share your problems with people who can help you solve that problem

Rule 24

BE HONEST

Dishonesty is like driving a car too fast; sooner or later you are going to slip off the road and crash.

Honesty, on the other hand, will take you where you want to go— safe and sound.

Salespeople already have the reputation of living in that "gray area." We need you to help change that! If you exaggerate or over promise and under deliver, you will always be letting people down.

ISLAND LORE

The Island doesn't tolerate anything but the truth. Yes, Colonel Jessup, we CAN handle the truth!

If you are managing salespeople and you notice you have someone who lies about little things, they probably lie about big things, too.

If they had a roast beef sandwich for lunch but tell you they had turkey … forget it. They can't be trusted.

Honesty is the only way to build a career, relationships and a life.

Rule 25
TAKE EXCELLENT NOTES

If you work in a position with high customer contact, make sure to take excellent notes on your prospects and reflect that information back to them.

The more personal your notes are, the more useful they will be.

On the phone, you probably have a CRM system that logs all of the applicable data needed to process a sale. That information is great, but just as important—if not more so— is the personal information that you can acquire yourself. Things like the soccer game that little Billy had, or the weekend getaway at the lake in three weeks.

ISLAND LORE

The weekend at the lake was lovely, thank you for asking.

"Hey, how did your son Billy do in his soccer game?"
"How was the weekend away at the lake? Did you get the rest you were hoping for?"

You may think you will remember everything, but you won't. Write it down and organize it!

*A study of 540 companies
conducted by the American
Society for Training and
Development shows that
continuous investments in
training and reinforcement
result in:*

- Over 50% higher net sales per employee
- Nearly 40% higher gross profits per employee

The same study found that leading-edge companies
spend 6% of payroll on learning and train almost 90%
of their employees during a given year.

Rule 26

ADULTS LEARN BY DOING

The best way you can learn something is by actually doing it. Reading books (like this one!) and learning about sales is great, but you need to put the lessons learned into action immediately.

Get comfortable with the fact that sooner or later, you need to play in the game. Practice is crucial, but game time is where you actually learn the most.

Don't be afraid to screw up. Everybody does. In fact, that is when you learn the most!

ISLAND LORE

The Island does not tolerate people afraid to make mistakes. We want risk-takers and doers!

To paraphrase Nike, just get in there and do it.

Think about professional athletes. They have a constant balance of practice and games. You learn how to perform under pressure in a game, and practice keeps you sharp.

We live for the game, so get in there as soon as you can.

Rule 27
DRESS TO IMPRESS

When you look great you feel great and when you feel great…you sell great!

Your presentation is not only what you say, it's just as much about how you look…WHILE you are saying it because it is all part of your presentation.

There is an old saying that says you should "always dress for the job you want, not the job you have."

You should always look your best, out dress your peers and look like a million bucks!

ISLAND LORE

We know that many startup companies (and also super cool places like Google) encourage very casual dress. Even in those situations, leaving your flip flops and wrinkled tee at home once in a while won't hurt.

Rule No. 27

Rule 28
NEVER INTERRUPT

Never interrupt your prospect. Let them finish their thoughts. It's crucial to talk WITH people, not AT people.

Sales should be a conversation, not a verbal assault.

Even if you know what's coming, LET THEM FINISH!

If you hurry them, they will hurry off.

ISLAND LORE

We keep a special boat on the Island for interrupters and it only goes one way—away.

Sometimes salespeople interrupt with an answer before the customer is done asking the question. You're not helping the process even though you feel like you are by saving time.

Even if you **think** you know what the customer was going to say (and you may be right), it's important for the customer that you actually **hear** it so that they know you understand.

People hate being interrupted.

Rule 29
BE PASSIONATE

Are you passionate about your product? If you are, then hopefully that passion shines through in your sales presentations.

But what if you AREN'T passionate about your product? Or your company?

Then you need to get passionate about the people you deal with and the conversations you have with them.

ISLAND LORE

Without passion, the Island is a cold, bleak place. It's the passion that brings the warm sun, refreshing breeze and steel drums.

Be passionate.

The more you love what you do, the better you will be at it.

If you're not passionate about what you do, then it's time to move on.

We always know when a salesperson is unhappy and nearing the end. It usually is directly tied to their passion—or lack thereof—for their career.

Rule 30
BOUNCE BACK TOMORROW

We like to talk about having a great attitude and handling the ebbs and flows of a sales career.

It's so important to bounce back from not only the lows, but from the highs, as well.

If you're extremely discouraged after missing a goal, you can take that night to be down. But be ready to bounce back to an even keel tomorrow.

ISLAND LORE

The longer you're in the game, the more you see how important this is. You have to learn how to leverage emotions—and the lack of emotions.

If you're No. 1 and you just crushed your quota and beat everyone globally in sales, allow yourself that night or weekend to celebrate. Then be sure to bounce back to your even keel tomorrow.

You cannot get too high or too low in sales. You must always bounce back to your even keel tomorrow.

If you are frustrated by a situation, your sales will suffer.

If you are fascinated by a situation, your sales will soar.

Rule 31

PLAY THE LAW OF AVERAGES

To be an above-average salesperson, you have to believe in the Law of Averages.

As you may recall from physics class, the Law of Averages states "a random event will 'even out' within a small sample."

Be logical. Every time you hear a "no," remind yourself that you're one step closer to a "yes."

Endure your bad days knowing that great days are right around the corner.

Trying a certain sales technique 3 times is not playing the law of averages. You have to commit.

Calling twenty people is not committing.

ISLAND LORE

He who bumps into enough palm trees is bound to get a coconut on the head.

Too many people jump ship before it has a chance to right its course and cruise on to The Island of Sales.

Rule 32

PREPARE, BUT NOT TOO MUCH

You should pride yourself on being well prepared. Your customers will expect it, and success in a sales career demands it.

Prepare quickly and thoroughly.

Be careful though: **One of the most common types of sales reluctance stems from over-preparation.**

For example: Mary loves to read about her leads in CRM for 7 minutes before picking up the phone to call them. Reading every last detail and communication log. If you have 60 leads to call every day that equals 7 hours of preparation. That is too much preparation.

ISLAND LORE

"Failure to prepare is preparing to fail."
—John Wooden

Be mindful of the time you spend preparing and make sure to not over-prepare. If you feel like preparing is a "safe activity" and you prefer it over calling, you are suffering from sales reluctance and need to call the Island of Sales hotline immediately!

So prepare, but not too much!

Rule 33

DUDE...ARE YOU...
TALKING TO ME?

Always wear a pinky ring, a gold chain and a big, gaudy watch.

You never know when someone might ask you for the time.

ISLAND LORE

Now go look in the mirror. Would you buy from you? Actually, let's rephrase: Would everyone else buy from you?

Rule No. 33

Rule 34
VISUALIZE SUCCESS

Visualizing success is a surefire way to increase your likelihood of success.

Most people think this is rubbish, that a way of thinking can't control results. Our advice to those who doubt is: Try it.

Try to be positive and visualize success for two straight months. We bet you will see results. If you don't, do it for 6 months and then a year… Let us know what those results are!

Visualizing can be done many different ways.
• Write down goals
• Hang up pictures of rewards you want

ISLAND LORE

On the Island, we visualize sun, waves and palm trees swaying in the breeze. For some reason, visualizing these things comes naturally.

The power of visualization is amazing. If you visualize bills and debt, you can expect more of that. If you visualize bonus checks and vacations, expect more of that!

Seems like an easy choice to us.

Rule 35
SET EXPECTATIONS

Set expectations up front.

Ask your prospect if they can give you a certain amount of time.

Ask them to tell you "no" if it's not a good match.

Tell them you want to spend the last five minutes of the call discussing next steps.

The clearer you are about your agenda and the more defined your prospect's expectations are, the more effective the conversation will be.

ISLAND LORE

You can expect three things on The Island: to have a good time, to work hard and to enjoy great success. We want to be up front about all of those things.

Rule 36

THE TWO-CHOICE RULE

"I'll take the red one. No, wait, the blue one. No, the YELLOW one. No ... wait!"

The more options you give someone, the harder it is to choose one.

Don't drown your prospects in an ocean of choices.

Whenever possible, try to give your customer two choices—and no more than that.

Yes or no?

3 or 4?

Tuesday or Wednesday?

Today or tomorrow?

ISLAND LORE

Would you like rum or whiskey? Let's keep it very simple. Although rum is popular on islands, we prefer Whiskey on ours!

Rule 37
BE RELIABLE

If you say you're going to do something, DO IT!

And if you say you're going to be
somewhere, BE THERE!

Be reliable and be a person of your
word. Hold yourself accountable
when you fail because the fastest
way to lose someone's trust is to
NOT be trustworthy.

ISLAND LORE

You can always rely on
The Island of Sales to
teach you how to sell and
increase your business

If you let your client down, you're only letting yourself down.

It's pretty simple.

The salesperson is the largest factor in a customer's decision to buy. The salesperson accounts for 39% of the decision, while price only accounts for 18%.

Rule 38
GET FIRED UP

If you sell, you need to be fired up. Not just about the product, but about life.

Ignite the people around you and the whole team catches fire.

This is a key factor not only in team success, but individual success as well.

Vince Lombardi said it best: "If you aren't fired with enthusiasm, you will be fired with enthusiasm."

We stand by that quote.

ISLAND LORE

If you get fired from the Island, you have to swim home. So get fired up, because the ocean is filled with sharks that love to eat non-fired up, lame people.

Rule No. 38

Rule 39
GET REFERRALS

If you don't have a steady flow of referrals, then something is wrong.

It either means that your product or service isn't valued (in which case you should sell something else), or it means you're not doing your job well enough.

Asking for referrals is something many salespeople hesitate to do or just don't make time for, but don't feel you are overstepping personal or professionals boundaries.

ISLAND LORE

You may have success in both life and in business, but you will have much more if you ask everyone for a referral.

Be proud of what you offer! Ask everyone for a referral.

Referrals convert at a higher percentage than any other lead source, so don't miss your opportunity.

Rule 40

ALWAYS GET A FIRM, FUTURE COMMITMENT

LET THE CHASE BEGIN!! Do you love chasing prospects as much as we do?

Leaving messages … leaving voicemails … not knowing if they got them … not knowing if they ever want to speak with you again?

We are in sales, not fortune telling or mind reading.

ISLAND LORE

I am free for the next 365 days. Just tell me what works for you! Sunday at 6 a.m.? Perfect!

Always mention to your customer that you know they are busy, and you would rather not pester them with calls, emails or unwanted visits.

Ask them if you can simply look at your respective calendars, pick a date and time to touch base again, and put it on your calendars.

They will agree most of the time, and you will be much more efficient!

Rule No. 40

Rule 41
LIE, CHEAT & STEAL

OK, OK, we know … very advanced and polished advice, huh? "Lie, cheat and steal." For real?

Look, there's no shame. It's smart.

If you experiencing an absolutely horrible day, week or month, sometimes you just have to lie to yourself. You have to convince yourself that things are OK and that you don't want to quit.

ISLAND LORE

This advice is so good, we should charge you for it … then steal it back.

Hopefully you never cheated off of anyone in school but if you did it surely wasn't off of the kid with the D-minus average. It's OK to cheat and steal in sales, however, just be sure to cheat off of the A-plus student, the person on your team who hits quota relentlessly. Copy what they say, copy how they say it and copy how they do it.

Look up at the sales leader board, find the person at the top and then do exactly what they're doing.

At some point you will make it yours, but when starting off look no further than the bright spots on your team.

Rule 42

REMEMBER NAMES

Rule #17 mentions that when someone hears their name, they listen more and they appreciate it.

The tricky part to this is that you can't use your prospect's name if you don't remember it.

Do whatever trick is necessary to remember customer's names!

Try this:
"Jim Jim bo bim, banana fanna fo fim, mee mi mo mim … Jiiiiiiiiiim."

Of course remembering the name is step 1. Using the name is step two. A chicken and egg situation.

ISLAND LORE

FDR was President of the United States. Kind of a busy job. He knew everyone by name—from the secret service agents to the doormen and mechanics. No excuses. If someone as busy as FDR is willing to do it, so can you!

Rule No. 42

HAVE FUN FIRST

In sales, it's important to have fun and THEN make money. Not the other way around.

Don't put the cart before the horse. Or in this case, the cart before the Porsche.

If you can have fun in your day-to-day calls, if you exude an energetic and enthusiastic attitude, you will make the type of money you are hoping for.

ISLAND LORE

Not to get all philosophical, but, isn't life supposed to be fun?

If you believe that once you start making money you will start having fun, you may never do either.

You have completed the first 43 Rules in The Pocket Guide For Sales Survival.

Before you "Check into Your Villa" and dig into the intermediate rules, here is a quick story about HAVING FUN and MAKING MONEY!

Having Fun Will Make You Money

HAVING FUN WILL MAKE YOU MONEY
By Jason DeAmato

The year was 2006 when I first learned how profitable having fun is. I owned and operated an outsourced customer acquisition firm, or simply put, an inside sales call center for hire. Our clients were businesses that wanted to ramp up their sales and marketing and would rely on us to do that. We had three clients over a two-year span. This story is about one particular client and his impact on my life. Specifically, about having fun and turning that into profit.

First, here is a little background on our client.

Jon, our client, was an interesting man. He was extremely intelligent and exceptionally funny. He was a workaholic. To say he was intimidating is an understatement. He would lure you in and charm you with his humor and charisma and then, when you were least expecting, and most expecting, he would make you want to run and hide. He had a way of making you love him, but also fear him twice as much as you loved him.

Jon's company was located across the street from my company, so unlike other clients who were in Atlanta and Los Angeles, he could pop in anytime. One thing was for sure—I wanted Jon staying on "his side of the street," and not popping in. When Jon walked into a room it felt like an old mafia movie. The mob boss walks through plumes of cigar smoke and nobody knows which poor guy is going to get whacked.

It was the first company I had started, and Randy, my business partner (and future co-author of The Pocket Guide to Sales Survival), was away for the week. It was hard enough running the business together 14 hours a day, so you can imagine a week without him.
We had started with just the two of us in a small basement (literally) and

now we had 15 employees and had developed from a company with nothing to a promising young startup.

We had grown exponentially, and so had Jon's company.

Mutually, we agreed on sales goals every week based on leads, growth projections and conversion rates.

At this point, our weekly sales goal was 50 sales per week. We usually hovered between 35-45 sales per week as a team, so 50 sales was aggressive and we knew it. For every sale my company made on behalf of Jon's company, we received a commission.

Although we grew to a million dollar company within 14 months, we were only six months in and still fighting to ramp up and fund our growth stage.

This story is about a specific week that was monumental in our company's history.

The best way to describe what happened this week is to walk through the days and hours as things unfolded. Here is a nice timeline of the most stressful week of my life, but also the most enlightening.

Monday 6:00pm (Sales Count = 3)

The first day of the week is complete and we booked a pathetic three deals. This is a disastrous first day. Typically, how you start the week will make or break your goal. Jon pays his first visit of the week. As the sales floor is clearing out, he saunters in wearing his black leather jacket.

Jon walks into my office and sits down. He just loved to sit back and not say anything for a good 45 seconds. He twirls around on the swivel chair and looks up and simply says, "Don't worry about the bad day, man. I have faith that you guys will kill it tomorrow."

I was so relieved that he wasn't telling me how terrible we were at sales or panicking about the weekly goal, suggesting we fire half of our employees. Although Jon was hard to work with and pushed us as hard as any client ever will, I learned so much from him and would not be where I am today without having worked with him. We chit chat and we both go home for the night.

Tuesday 8:00 am (Sales Count = 3)
The sales floor gathered around their cubes for the morning sales meeting. I summarized Monday and quickly tell them to shake it off. We got to work.

Tuesday 12:00 pm (Sales Count = 4)
Things are not improving and the moments are quickly ticking away. I am not happy but have faith we will pick it up. In the meantime, I am hoping Jon stays away.

Tuesday 3:00 pm (Sales Count = 5)
Oh no. We should have 20 sales by now and I am starting to have that feeling. You know the feeling, I'm falling from a plane heading straight towards rocky earth at 600 miles per hour without a parachute. Yes, that feeling.

Tuesday 6:00 pm (Sales Count = 5)
Day 2 is complete and the disastrous sales week is looking like a certainty. I blast out of work so fast, praying not to see Jon crossing the street as I head for my car. I make it out alive ... phew. I ruined dinner that night as I just kept asking my wife, how could we do three sales on Monday

and two today? She tells me things will work out. I go to sleep somewhat unconvinced they will.

Wednesday 12:00 pm (Sales Count = 5)
This is officially a nightmare. We are 20 deals behind where we need to be and the week is half over. Sales are just not coming in and our goal is 50 sales!

Wednesday 3:00 pm (Sales Count = 7)
Jon walks in the office like Mike Tyson would, looking for the guy who ran over his puppy. He comes right into my office but this time he doesn't sit. He shuts the door and turns his back to me looking through the glass window and peering out at the sales floor.

Jon: "What's going on, Man? I am getting pretty nervous. We're almost halfway through the week and you are not even close to the goal."
Me: "This is sales, Man. Sometimes this happens. There are ebbs and flows."
Jon: "Do you really believe that?" He says in the most condescending tone humanly possible. "Because I'll tell you what I see. I see a bunch of losers that couldn't close a door if I held their hand and pushed. I could come over here and sell more deals by myself than your whole floor could. This is bullshit. You better get your act together man, because I hate losing, I will not lose. If I have to come over here and sell myself I will. You call this a sales company?"

He slammed the door as he walked out.

I sat in my chair for a minute and thought about what to do. Jon knew his rant would force me to take action. He was no dummy, and knew I was just as upset as he was at the impending failure. This was his way of getting me fired up. So, although I disagree with his approach, and would never manage my staff that way, I give him credit because it

Having Fun Will Make You Money

worked. I knew there were two choices:

1. Go out there and make it happen
2. Let this situation gain momentum and possibly watch my company implode

I walked out onto the floor and yelled for everyone's attention.

Silence. And then I gave the most explosive speech of my life. It had to be.

I paced back and forth with motivating stories about success and believing until the final bell rings. I could not have been more sincere and heartfelt. This was my life, this company was my baby, and we had to fight to save it. Nothing in life comes easy.

Here is an excerpt from the end of that speech:

"We need to get 50 sales. It is almost 4 o'clock on Wednesday and we have 7 sales. Nobody believes in us. The guy across the street definitely doesn't, and he thinks he can outsell all of us put together. Even I didn't believe in us this morning, but right now I do. We are doing this. That's it. Our mission from now until Saturday at 5pm is to **have fun**. There is one **mandatory** rule … you have to have fun. So, either have fun or get fired. Who is ready to hit 50 sales? The comeback of a lifetime starts right now, and it starts with us having a blast! Turn the music up and let's DO THIS!!"

Of course, nobody left and everyone screamed with me.

The most important thing I did that day, right after screaming like William Wallace in front of the entire company, was that I walked over to my office, but did not go in. Instead, I closed the door and locked it and then sat right smack in the middle of the sales floor and yelled "Who's got a lead for me? Anyone I close, you get the credit if you give me the lead."

Before I could sit down, I had Andy's lead sheet on my desk with 10 names from Texas. I picked up the phone and started selling. I had 40 leads on my desk within five minutes. Perfect!

For the next three hours we had more fun selling than ever before. Every customer became a friend, every deal felt like a million dollar deal.

Wednesday 6:00 pm (Sales Count = 11)
We closed four more deals on Wednesday. It wasn't a huge day but at least there was some movement. We knew we still had to pull off a heroic comeback.

Thursday 8:00 am (Sales Count =11)
Thursday morning, one of our true sales leaders, Andrew Cleak, pointed out to me that everyone was ready to rock. I walked around the room and welcomed people back. Then I looked in everyone's eyes; they had listened … they were going to have fun.

That day we cranked music, threw the ball around, got rid of our chairs so that everyone was standing while selling, pushed, shoved, told jokes, made fun of each other and did just about everything a sales floor can to have fun.

If anyone had walked into this room you would have felt it. It is hard to explain what it felt like other than the room caught energy tantamount to a blistering inferno.

Literally, it felt like nothing I have ever experienced.

Having Fun Will Make You Money

Thursday 6:00 pm (Sales Count = 34)
Woah!

Friday 6:00 pm (Sales Count = 57)
Are you serious?

Saturday 5:00 pm (Sales Count = 73)
We didn't hit our goal, we destroyed it.

Demolished it.

We crushed 50 sales and went on to our biggest and most profitable week yet.

Why did this happen?

We were so determined to have fun that we lit ourselves on fire and our customers ignited too. The atmosphere was so engaging in the room that our customers had to be a part of whatever we were doing and therefore they bought, and bought, and bought.

They felt our energy through the phone.

From 11 sales on Wednesday to 73 on Saturday.

What I saw with my own two eyes, what I will never forget, was people enjoying every second of it.
Looking back, this was the theme of our entire company.

We didn't have the best salespeople in the world, or fancy CRM's and IT resources, not even close. But what we did have was unparalleled energy, and it stemmed from having FUN.

Having Fun Will Make You Money

If you don't believe it, try it.

-Jason DeAmato

Intermediate

CHECKING INTO YOUR VILLA

Rule 44
HAVE A PROCESS

Learn a sales process.
Here's an example of a simple sales process that we have used and built companies around:

- Prepare
- Introduce
- Investigate and Understand
- Consult and Present
- Close
- Summarize

If you don't follow a sales process, you're dismissing the science of communication.

Having a solid sales process ensures you will be leveraging the psychology of sales and communication.

ISLAND LORE

When you sell without a process you usually end up lost. The problem is nobody is there to give you directions. You just end up driving in circles until you run out of gas.

Having a process also allows you to focus on more advanced skills. If your sales process is second nature, you can free up the needed mental bandwidth to understand and practice advanced sales techniques.

If you are without a process and thinking about "where do I go next?" you cannot focus on advanced techniques.
It is very fitting to start the "Intermediate" chapter with this rule.

It is our way of stressing just how important it is. It was either this, or name the book "Have a Process" but Island of Sales has more of a ring to it.

Rule 45
BUILD LASTING RELATIONSHIPS

You can't marry a pair of jeans, but you can marry the person who sells them to you.

Wait. What was that?

It's simple: People connect with people first and foremost. Build a relationship and you will be exponentially closer to a sale.

It's very common to see new salespeople who have been inundated with training, product knowledge and new surroundings fall victim to the "it" sale. They focus on whatever the product or service is and they sell "it."

It's equally common for veteran salespeople who are very good at matching needs or providing solutions for pain points to only sell the product and service that "solves problems."

Don't forget to sell yourself! Great rapport-builders who also focus on moving the sale forward are usually the best closers on the floor.

Relationship building will separate you from the pack.

As an added bonus, relationships are the key to networking, referrals, and overall business success.

You would feel much better going into battle with someone you know has your back than you would a stranger.

Rule No. 45

Use that same rationale and apply to sales. A customer feels more apt to buy something from someone they feel has their back.

Make connections, care about the results, and relationships will happen.

ISLAND LORE

We value relationships so much that we built an Island to foster them forever! That's right, we've got your back!

GRAIN OF SAND:

Technology is making relationships more important than ever. Information is free and just a click away.

Excellent customer service is absolutely the key to differentiating yourself from competition.

Rule 46
BUILD TRUST

Sometimes all you have in sales is trust.

The prospects have to trust that what you are telling them is true and that your product is the right one for them.

As soon as you have achieved this trust in the sales process, the selling is over. So tell the truth and it will show.

ISLAND LORE

Do you always do what you say you are going to do?

Don't just build trust **initially**; make sure you foster that trust throughout the duration of your relationship.

It's sad that people have to be reminded to be trustworthy, but unfortunately, snake oil salesmen still exist.

There is a better way. Trust us.

Rule No. 46

BE A STUDENT OF THE GAME

If you're like most salespeople, you've probably earned a large amount of your success on your own. That doesn't mean there's nothing left to learn or nothing to improve upon.

Be a great student. Study the psychology of sales and learn from the people around you.

You may be a "born" salesperson with a "natural" gift of persuasion, but there are always behaviors and techniques that are missing from your repertoire. Identify them and learn them!

The difference between GOOD and GREAT is slight. If you can consistently learn how to do just a little bit more, you will consistently be just a little bit better!

ISLAND LORE

Albert Einstein said, "Once you stop learning, you start dying." For that wisdom, we'll make him an honorary member of the Island.

No matter how much money you make or how experienced you are, you should always seek out new information. The day you stop improving your craft is the day you're surpassed by someone who does. Be the person who goes the extra mile to continue learning.

Pick up a book (like this one!) and put down the remote.
Instead of surfing the web for things you can't afford, search the web to learn new ways to become a better salesperson.

Rule 48

DON'T FIND A WAY ... MAKE A WAY!

Your career will be filled with moments when victory seems impossible and defeat seems inevitable. There are many different road blocks and challenges that you simply have to overcome.

Many times the path to success won't be clear and defined. When faced with such a moment, what will you do? Will you wait for someone else to come to the rescue? Or will you press on and blaze a new path for yourself?

> ## ISLAND LORE
>
> We didn't find the Island, we created it!

There is a way—there is always a way. If you can't find it, then create it.

Some of the toughest challenges you will face may be caused by others, but don't ever forget that anytime you point a finger, there are three pointing right back at you (Go ahead, try it!).

Go **make** your way.

GET UNCOMFORTABLE

Closing is rarely comfortable. So get comfortable being uncomfortable.

The times in business, and in life, where you are most uncomfortable are absolutely the times you are learning and growing the most.

We love salespeople for this very reason. Salespeople don't want comfort. Elite salespeople don't get uncomfortable or thrown off when they find themselves in unchartered territory or new challenging situations…they thrive on it!

Step out of your comfort zone every chance you get.

ISLAND LORE

We have so many uncomfortable situations on the Island that every day we all bow down to a statue of Larry David. Pretty, prettaaay good!

Get uncomfortable.

Rule 50
NUMBERS GAME

You will hear every cliché in the world. People telling you to grind it out and put in the hours.

There is a reason you hear all of those clichés: because they are true. Never forget the importance of hard work and the process of finding **quality in quantity**.

Every sales industry has its own cycle and conversion rates. Be ready to crank and work harder than everyone else, and you will find success.

ISLAND LORE

We tried using the numbers game at the blackjack table once. $12,000 later, we agreed: It works! Vegas, baby!

This is similar to Rule #3, but here we are talking about figuring out the numbers and attacking. I need to call 100 people in order to talk to 10 in order to close two. Then, there I go!

I now know what I need to do every day to close two people a day. One hundred calls! That is called working the numbers game.

Rule 51
SPEAK NATURALLY

You should always talk to people as if they're already a friend or family member. Your tone of voice should be natural. This requires practice and (usually) some coaching.

We love training people on tone of voice. They'll read a script and sound like a "telemarketer reading from a script." Big shock, huh?

Then when they're done reading they speak with a normal tone again. What just happened? Why did you change when you were reading?

You should talk to clients and prospects with the same **tone** that you do your co-workers or friends. What you say changes. How you say it should remain consistent.

With clients be **professional** and **natural**.

Be natural in your tone and conversations and you will be in like Flynn.

Rule 52
BE KNOWLEDGEABLE

Know your stuff.

No excuses.

How can you tell a prospect that
your product or service is right for
them if they have questions about it
that you can't answer?

There's nothing more comforting
for a buyer than to be in the hands
of a knowledgeable, confident
salesperson who's an expert in their
trade.

ISLAND LORE

"Ahh ... umm ... I'm not
quite sure what the Lore
is for this entry. Let me
check with someone here
and I'll get back to you on
that one."

Use cheat sheets, pick the brains of the top performers, research
competitors, do a lunch and learn each week, listen to other reps on the
phone and again, know your stuff. When a customer senses that you
don't, that is when they usually stop listening.

Rule No. 52

Rule 53
BE ORGANIZED

Highly organized people work faster and more efficiently than disorganized people.

Organize everything. Your desk, your computer files, your phone numbers ... scripts, cheat sheets, emails, email templates, product specs, leads, follow ups....

You can never be too organized.

If organization isn't your thing, make it your thing. Otherwise your disorganization will rob you of much-needed time.

ISLAND LORE

It's funny that another word for "company" is "organization," and yet some of those "organizations" have no organization. Try saying that 10 times fast!

ASK GREAT QUESTIONS

An easy way to tell the difference between a seasoned veteran and a sales rookie is simple: The rookie talks and the veteran listens.

When you ask your prospects great questions, you'll get the exact information you need to get the sale.

Prepare your list of great questions, then sit back and listen!

ISLAND LORE

Where were you last night between the hours of 11 p.m. and 1:30 a.m.? Answer the question!

Don't ask too many questions, though. You don't want to make the prospect feel like they are on the witness stand.

Rule 55
SELL

Technology is great. Software is great. There are some fantastic tools available these days to help facilitate the sales process.

There are programs that manage your customer base, educate you on competition; forecast new business ... the list goes on.

Just remember: Through all of the clicks, opens and saves, don't forget to **pick up the phone, or knock on the door and SELL!**

> ### ISLAND LORE
>
> Wait, I actually have to sell and close deals? I can't just blast emails to prospects all day? I didn't sign up for this...

Don't let technology dehumanize your sales process. Leverage technology, sure, but stay true to the human aspect of sales.

Hesitation to get down to the nitty gritty can cost you a few sales, and a few sales can cost you the President's Club.

Rule 56
LEARN OUTSIDE THE OFFICE

Two concepts here:

• Take **home** the same concepts you deal with at work. This allows you to access different parts of your brain on the same problems.
• Go outside your office to learn new concepts, philosophies and ways to enhance you and your company.

Concept 1:

We all get our fair share of knowledge and wisdom, in the office, but what about when we go home? We act different, feel different and certainly think different at home. You may not notice these subtle changes, but once you embrace them, it is a game-changer.

Try taking the same concept that has been giving you trouble at the office for a week, and bringing it home for a night. You may find an answer before you even open the laptop. In the comfort of your home, you may get the clarity that you need.

Concept 2:

In the office you don't get to choose who teaches you!

So what happens if you do not connect with them?

The beauty of learning from outside of work is that you get to choose the book, podcast, blog, video or seminar that CONNECTS WITH YOU!

If you start reading a book and it doesn't connect, you are better off finding one you connect with right away and keeping it close by at all times.

Outside seminars and team-building exercises are perfect examples of how to implement new concepts and philosophies. Getting people outside of the office to build relationships and learn different things that are not taught in the office works.

ISLAND LORE

If you are reading this, you pass!

Don't wait for your company to offer these things. Do it on your own!

Without follow up, salespeople will lose 80-90 percent of what they learned in training within just one month!

All sales training programs should include follow up reinforcement and/or coaching by the training team, sales managers or both.

This follow up is key to leveraging the investment in training, increasing retention and improving sales performance.

Fact No. 2

Rule 57
REACT TO BUYING SIGNS

Buying signs! What do they look like? What do they sound like? When do they strike?

Buying signs come in all shapes and sizes. Some are obvious while some are subtle. Learn to recognize them by paying attention to your customers. Even if a sale doesn't happen, you can still gain some newfound knowledge about buying signs from the exchange.

Buying signals can be physical or verbal cues that a prospect sends that indicate interest. Very rarely will you hear, "Great, can I buy this from you now, pleeeease?"

ISLAND LORE

There are two things we don't joke about on the Island. One is sniffing out buying signs. The other is short people. We don't find them funny at all. They're just short. Except Martin Short. He's funny and short.

When you see a buying sign, and it feels like an appropriate moment … go for the close.

Knowing when your customer is ready to buy is crucial to closing sales. If you try to close too early, you come across as too aggressive. If you wait too long, you could miss the boat! Remember, buying signs can crop up in the first few minutes, so be ready for them!

Some basic buying signs are questions about product variation such as whether it comes in a different color or style.

Make sure to listen for questions about warranty, start of service, delivery date, contract specifics, price or mode of payment.

Rule 58
WANT IT

How bad do you want it?

If you "kind of" want to be No. 1 in your office, you may get there.
Eventually. With a little luck.

If you're "dying" to be No. 1, your odds are a hell of a lot better.

Can you hear the difference?

Feeling genuine passion about reaching your goals is much better
motivation than doing it simply because someone else told you to.

Want it for you!

ISLAND LORE

The next time you have 10 free minutes, read "The Little Engine
That Could." Sure, you know the story. Sure, you've heard it a
million times. But, when was the last time? Go read it. I think you
can ... I think you can ... I think you can ...

Rule 59

HOLD YOURSELF ACCOUNTABLE

This person:

- Lost his job in 1832.
- Was defeated for state legislature in 1832.
- He failed in business in 1833.
- His sweetheart died in 1835.
- He had nervous breakdown in 1836.
- Was defeated for speaker in 1838.
- Was defeated for nomination for congress in 1843.
- Rejected for congress in 1848.
- Rejected for land officer in 1849.
- Defeated for U.S. senate in 1854.
- Defeated for nomination for vice president in 1856.
- Defeated again for U.S. senate in 1858...

But...

In 1860, the man we all know as Abraham Lincoln was elected president of the United States of America and went on to successfully lead his country through its greatest constitutional, military and moral crisis in history. Lincoln preserved the union while ending slavery and becoming one of the most memorable and respected presidents in history.

Lincoln is consistently ranked in the top three, often #1, of all time presidents in popularity and accomplishments.

When it comes to accountability, you need to acknowledge the wins and the losses.

It is crucial to hold yourself accountable for failures, learn from those mistakes and then "keep on, keeping on."

You never know, if you continue to hold yourself accountable...the very next time you make an attempt at something, might just be your "1860."

ISLAND LORE

Hold yourself accountable for your wins and your losses! You might be surprised at the lessons you will uncover when you look in the mirror and relish in your failures...

Rule No. 59

Rule 60
BE A GREAT TEAMMATE

Sales is a lot like baseball. It's a very individualistic game made up of one-on-one match-ups, but the sum of those individual match-ups equals a total team effort.

And you need to be a good teammate.

Nobody is going to help you hit the ball or close a sale in the heat of the moment.

ISLAND LORE

We are certainly two guys who believe in teamwork. Years ago, someone pointed out to us that 1 + 1 does not always equal 2. Sometimes 1 + 1 equals a lot more than that.

However, the better a teammate you are, the better individual contributor you become.

Being a great teammate means learning, motivating, mentoring and sharing your invaluable intangibles.

Rule 61
KEEP YOUR WORD

You will make mistakes. Promise the wrong price … Double book yourself for appointments …

No matter what the error is, always try to keep your word.

It may mean you have to give up some commission or stay late to make up for your mistake.

Take your medicine and learn for the next time.

ISLAND LORE

We give you our word to always keep it short and simple. If we don't, we'll put the rest in "Island Lore."

Rule No. 61

Rule 62
KNOW YOUR COMPETITION

It's essential to have a deep understanding of your competition and the industry you share.

You should not only know the cons to every competitor, but the pros as well.

When discussing competition, make sure you mention their positives—albeit with a healthy dose of indifference.

Yes!

It says a lot about you and your product, when you aren't afraid to point out competitor strengths.

Rule 63

TALK WITH DECISION-MAKERS

The first step is getting to the decision-maker. Once you're there, you're on your own!

Just kidding. We can help with that too!

The first thing to remember is that decision-makers are just like everyone else. They have hopes and dreams and fears and insecurities. However, when you're dealing with the decision-maker, it's particularly important to know what type of personality you're dealing with.

ISLAND LORE

Alright, attention, everyone! I have one question before I get started: which one of you is the decision maker?

If it's the bossy, controlling type, just give the facts. Keep it short and simple. Let them do what they do, which is make decisions. If it's the very emotional type, you should tell stories and use testimonials. Share ideas and feelings.

If it's someone in between controlling and emotional, give them in between. Just understand your customer.

Rule No. 63

Rule 64
JONES THEORY

Everyone wants to be like the Joneses. So you should talk about other customers that are already using the product and the benefits they are experiencing.

Keeping up with the Joneses –

To "keep up with the Joneses" is a common phrase used in America to convey the idea of people's desires, to do what others are doing and have what others are having.

We've all experienced "Keeping up with the Joneses" moments at some time in our life.

When talking with customers in ANY sales environment, it's important to recognize these opportunities and mention the people already enjoying and benefiting from your product or service.

ISLAND LORE

Oh, look who just arrived on the Island. It's the Jones family! And they brought everyone from your company, along with all your friends, family and neighbors. Everyone you know just arrived … why aren't you here?

Rule 65
BE SINCERE

Mean what you say.

If you don't believe it, don't say it.

Be sincere about your career.

If you are not sincere about your career, make a change!

This rule is short and simple, but so sincere.

ISLAND LORE

Sincerely, Jason and Randy

Rule 66
BELIEVE IN YOUR PRODUCT

Whenever possible, you should use your own product or service.

Try it, taste it, wear it, drive it, use it, and then stand up and be proud!

You absolutely have to believe in your own product or service. How can you get someone else to believe in your product if you don't?

Showing someone you believe in your product is conveyed through enthusiasm, proof, data, facts, knowledge, and many other factors.

ISLAND LORE

If you don't believe in your product, then you need to become a really good liar. Once you've mastered that, get off our Island before we throw you off.

So it is simple: when you love your product the chances of your customer loving it increase.

Rule 67

TURN FRUSTRATION INTO FASCINATION

To find true success and longevity in a sales career, you have to see obstacles as nothing more than interesting opportunities. Instead of being frustrated with not hitting quota, get fascinated with it instead.

Think of the situation as a homicide scene, and you're the ultra-cool CSI detective in the $300 sunglasses. There's your recent failure lying on the floor in a pool of blood, surrounded by a chalk outline. Now it's your job—your obsession—to find out how and why it happened.

When you're fascinated with why you didn't hit quota and you inquisitively try to get to the bottom of it, you will be pleasantly surprised when you find out why.

ISLAND LORE

Henry Ford once said, "Obstacles are those frightful things you see when you take your eyes off your goal." We imagine he said this while driving a Model-T past a field of grazing cows. "Mooooove!"

Change the way you look at things; this is something you can start doing immediately.

Rule No. 67

Rule 68

SACRIFICE, TO HIT YOUR GOALS

Creating more success in your career may mean less recreational time. Writing your own book may require less TV. Being closer to your children may require adjusting your work or social activities.

If your life (and your time) is already maxed out, there's no room for something new.

ISLAND LORE

Sacrifice bunts really do work in baseball. Every now and then you have to give up a hit in order to score a run.

Take a look at everything that fills up your daily schedule now and move some things around.

Re-prioritize.

Goals that require sacrifice and maybe even a little pain are the best types to have!

Rule 69

FOCUS ON YOUR GOALS EVERY DAY

Once you know what your goals are, think about them every day. Talk about them, write them down and share them with people.

Making your goals known to others adds an element of accountability to them. Even a little pressure.

Keeping your goals to yourself, on the other hand, might make you less inclined to work as hard as you can to reach them. After all, you're the only one who will know if you fail.

You'll be surprised how many more goals you achieve when you make sharing them a daily activity.

ISLAND LORE

Imagine if basketball courts had no hoops? Players would just run around in circles the entire game passing the ball to each other. Ever feel like you're just running around in circles? Throw a goal at each end of the court ... Game changer!

Rule No. 69

Rule 70
BUILD VALUE

Chances are, your prospect will have an idea of what your product or service is. But they need to see value in YOU as well.

Building value is crucial. Build value in both you and what you offer.

Chances are you have competition. Separate yourself and your services by educating your prospects on what makes you—and your product or service— different.

This is true value building!

Also, whenever possible, never mention price until you're sure the customer understands the value.

ISLAND LORE

If you build it, they will come.

Value! Value! Value!

We said it three times (with exclamation marks) to show just how important it is!

GRAIN OF SAND:

Sales managers that produce in the top 10% spend 66% of their time coaching on sales

GET THROUGH THE GATEKEEPERS

No matter who the client is, you're bound to encounter gatekeepers.

When you're dealing with a company, it's usually the receptionist, coldly swatting salespeople away like flies. But customers have gatekeepers, too. Maybe it's the husband who screens the sales call for his wife (who is the real decision-maker of the household).

Getting past a gatekeeper is an important but ominous task. If you want the sale, you must be creative, assertive, and even relentless.

Bring them a cake that reads, "Enrolling in our program is a piece of cake." Leave a baseball signed with a note that says, "I can't wait to give you my pitch."

There are millions of ways to step outside the box. When it comes to getting past the gatekeepers, you must LIVE outside the box!

ISLAND LORE

The Island has a gatekeeper, but they are pretty easy to circumvent. When they greet you at the dock, just give them a big smile and a friendly pat on the back. Oh, and a great ice breaker doesn't hurt either.

Gatekeepers can be tough, but don't forget that they are only people. The best way to get past them is to simply get close to them.

Rule 72
SMOKE OUT OBJECTIONS

Smoke out your prospects' hesitations or objections.

Always push to find out what seems to be holding someone back.

Without a clearly defined objection, there is no clearly defined solution.

Remember that most people will not volunteer negative information. You will need to smoke it out if you sense it's there.

ISLAND LORE

On the Island, objections are smoked out before we eat. Then we use that smoke to flavor the scotch of course.

Make it easy for people to say what's bothering them. We believe that most of the clients that fall into the "black hole" of sales had some form of an objection that was never brought to the surface.

Smoke it out ... then overturn it!

Rule 73

LEVERAGE THE SENSE OF URGENCY

You set the pace.

Unlike fine wine, "potential sales" only get worse with time, never better. That's why it's important to not let them go stale or get cold.

It's important to leverage the "sense of urgency" with your customer. This means that there's importance in the customer doing this NOW as opposed to later. You will see this advertised as:
• "This weekend only"
• "Blow-out sale"
• "1-day sale"

ISLAND LORE

If you use urgency carelessly, it will cost you sales. Use it early in the process to ensure consistency and make sure you "sense" it.

Most industries have legitimate reasons why acting fast is better than waiting. If you are in this space you must leverage the urgency.

You should, however, never manifest or try to "create" urgency that doesn't exist. This is a sure fire way to lose customers.

Rule No. 73

Rule 74
PITCH EVERYONE!

So now that you have made it past the gatekeeper, what next? It's time to speak with the decision-maker. But what if there are two (or more) decision-makers?

In these cases, you must pitch everyone. Don't make the mistake of explaining your product to one decision-maker and relying on them to explain it to someone else.

There is no way they will have the same impact that you do. Chances are you are explaining this for the 600th time, while they will be explaining it for the first time.

You want to control everything in the sales process, so if you let decision-maker No. 1 make the pitch to decision-maker No. 2, you're relying on someone less qualified to close your deal.

ISLAND LORE

Pitching two or three people at once will keep you on your toes. Kind of like when you're walking over hot coals for your Island initiation, although there are no hot coals here, just warm sand.

Get all the decision-makers involved as early as possible and pitch them at the same time. Control the situation.

Rule 75

PRACTICE ... NOT A GAME ... PRACTICE!

Contrary to Allen Iverson's famous rant, practice is pretty damn important.

In any line of work that involves a performance of some type—sports, theater, dance, music, cooking, surgery, NASA, sales—practice is paramount.

And yet in sales, practice is something people usually leave in the new-hire training room.

Big mistake.

You have to practice. To help you do so, here's a list of things to work on:

- Tone
- Product or service description
- Overturning objections
- Opening lines
- Ice breakers
- Closing
- Strategic questionings
- Leverage the sense of urgency
- Making a group presentation

ISLAND LORE

If it's not perfect, we will perfect it.

Once you sound great with something in practice, move on to the next thing.

Rule 76

DON'T WORRY ABOUT ANYTHING

In sales, you have probably been told that you shouldn't worry about the things you can't control. You know, things like the weather and your territory. These are, typically, things that you have no control over.

We agree with that and we also think that you shouldn't worry about the things you can control either.

You really shouldn't worry about anything, although you should care about all of it.

You should care greatly about your work ethic, your goals, your attitude, etc.

BE PERSISTENT

Wayne Gretzky, aka "The Great One," once said, "You miss 100% of the shots you don't take."

We couldn't have said it better ourselves, Wayne. Be persistent—not just in sales, but also in life.

You will be tested. You will want to give up. You will feel like giving up is the only option.

Stay the course and be persistent. Take shots. Persistence pays.

ISLAND LORE

Chicken Soup for the Soul was rejected 140 times and has now sold over 180 million copies. Imagine if the author had given up after the 139th rejection?

Rule No. 77

Rule 78
WATCH YOUR TONE

Connecting with your customers is largely a result of tonality.

Watch your tone. The inflection in your voice will captivate your prospect and set the tone for your entire conversation. Everyone involved should feel good. People make good decisions when they feel relaxed and comfortable.

ISLAND LORE

On the Island, everyone is like Stevie Wonder—all about perfect tone.

A great tone can inspire desirable emotional responses in your prospects and, emotional responses are huge in human decision-making.

Most of the techniques you will perform are of little value if your tone is off, and in sales, tone can be EVERYTHING.

Read these identical sentences and emphasize the bold word.

I didn't say that our competitor's product was better.
I **didn't** say that our competitor's product was better.
I didn't **say** that our competitor's product was better.
I didn't say **that** our competitor's product was better.
I didn't say that **our** competitor's product was better.
I didn't say that our **competitor's** product was better.
I didn't say that our competitor's **product** was better.
I didn't say that our competitor's product **was** better.
I didn't say that our competitor's product was **better**.

Rule 79
ALWAYS CHECK IN

Is that fair? May I proceed? Should I continue? Does that make sense? Do you have any questions about that?

These are things you should always be asking your customers.

Make sure to check in early and often during your presentations.

ISLAND LORE

By the way, how is the reading going? Are you loving this or what? We were hoping you would say that!

If customers are hearing something for the first time, chances are they may have questions.

The key is to bring your customer along for the ride; don't leave them behind.

Consistent "check ins" will ensure this!

Rule 80
BE PERSONABLE

Nobody likes to talk to a cold
product pusher. Be a real person.

- Talk about why you love the
  product
- Ask questions to understand your
  customer's motivation
- Inquire and get to know the person
  - Use their name
  - Use YOUR name
  - Humanize yourself with humor and humility

Remember: it's people, not products.

Rule 81

IDENTIFY AND ADMIT YOUR WEAKNESSES

Why are we so afraid to hear negative things about ourselves? Do we really think we are perfect?

Nobody is perfect, of course, but you can certainly strive for perfection. In doing so, you have to be willing to identify and admit to your weaknesses.

When is the last time you asked someone to help identify some of your weaknesses?

ISLAND LORE

One of our weaknesses is that we talk too much. OK, now it's your turn. What's one or two of your weaknesses?

More importantly, when they gave you their opinion of your weaknesses, how did you react?

Unless you ADMIT THEM, you cannot work on them.

Ask others where you could use some improvement or instruction, then swallow your pride and admit it.

Rule No. 81

Rule 82

LEAVE YOUR MESSAGE AT THE BEEP!

There's usually only one objective for a salesperson leaving a voicemail: to get a call back. Nothing more!

Be creative, but don't talk too much.

- Leave your name and number twice (once at the beginning of the message and once at the end)
- Create a reason for them to call you back by creating curiosity
- Speak slowly but with enthusiasm
- Talk to the voicemail like it's a real person you've known for years

ISLAND LORE

Seriously, have you ever listened to a voicemail from someone selling something? Don't you hit delete as soon as they say WHY they're calling?

If you tell someone why you are calling, they can decide if it's worth their time to call you back. If you say something like, "I have a quick question for you," it creates curiosity and the impulse to call back.

Rule 83
FOLLOW UP

Set dates and times for following up.
Then follow up.

The best salespeople are obsessive
about following up.

You don't really expect your
prospects to call you back, do you?

Call them!

ISLAND LORE

Following up is like
mowing the lawn. You
really don't like doing it,
but the more you mow, the
easier it is to maintain a
picture-perfect landscape.

*P.S. If you are not good with follow up,
make yourself a note, and be sure to
follow up with that!*

Rule No. 83

Rule 84
OVERTURNING OBJECTIONS

"Not tonight, honey, I have a headache."

Hopefully you're not thoroughly familiar with that classic objection to intimacy, but either way, you know what we're talking about.

What makes that objection so classic is that it's usually untrue. They don't really have a headache; they just don't want to give you a real reason for rolling over and going to sleep.

In sales, as in your everyday life, people will hesitate to tell you their true hesitations. So before you can overturn an objection, you have to determine if it's legit.

There are three simple rules when it comes time to overturning objections: **empathize, relate and solve**.

• Use empathy first. Let them know you hear their concerns.
• Next, relate to them. Tell them they're not the first customer to have these concerns.
• Finally, solve the issue. Educate your customer on why their objection, in this given scenario, should not be a concern.

Just remember to use a healthy amount of indifference when overturning objections. You don't want to come off desperate. Instead, have the detached air of a consultant. Talk like a consultant. Act like a consultant.

If you do get the true objections to the surface, overturn them and move quickly to your close. If you have a product or service that meets the customer's needs and there are no objections, it's already time to close.

Headache gone!

Rule No. 84

FOLLOW THE LEADER

We all played this game when we were young, and it's no different in your sales career.

Every sales industry and organization has their leaders.

Follow them!

ISLAND LORE

The best leaders know when it's time to follow, and when it's time to lead.

You don't have to reinvent the wheel to have major success in sales.

You should always try to emulate the successful people around you and follow their lead.

Someday, people will be following you.

Rule 86
STEP ON THE SCALE CLOSE

There are easily 200 different closing techniques, but until "The Pocket Guide for Closing Deals" is published, we want to start you off with one.

We like this because it is assertive, yet with the correct tone, can be very refreshing for a customer.

"Mr. Customer, before we get off the phone today, I'm wondering if you can tell me one thing: On a scale of 1 to 5, 1 being we aren't a match and 5 being you would sign an order form today, where would you say we are?"

ISLAND LORE

Please promise us you won't ever call someone "Mr. Customer." Unless, of course, that really is their last name.

Asking your prospect to rate the likelihood of moving forward sounds pretty blunt, doesn't it?

But it's also a clever way to ask for business because you are encouraging the customer to be honest.

Use it.

Rule No. 86

Rule 87
LEVERAGE THE FEAR OF LOSS

A prospect should always be reminded of what it's like without the product and what it would be like with the product.

Marketing experts will tell you one of the ways to get your prospects to buy from you is by tapping into their "fear of loss."

ISLAND LORE

We also know that not every situation lends itself to creating fear of loss, so only use it when the situation dictates.

Many experts believe marketing into your prospect's fear of loss is a lot more effective than marketing into their opportunity of gaining something. You will see this advertised as:

• "Only 3 items left!"
• "Stock is running out!"
• "Limited number available!"

Rule 88

TALK BEFORE YOU TEXT

When my generation was young, we came home when the street lights came on. Not when our mothers texted us—because there were no cell phones!

When we had social challenges, we had to actually talk to people about it. You had to talk to your teachers, neighbors or your girlfriend's parents. You couldn't send an email, text or update your status to communicate.

We were forced to develop social and communication skills by facing those tough situations.

ISLAND LORE

Ma u were kinda rude 2 Johnny last nite. Wat up w/ dat? LOL luv u - ttyl. lmao

Force yourself to talk to people, especially about the sensitive topics that require extreme focus on tone, content and body language.

Those discussions will prepare you for successful sales communication.

Rule No. 88

Approximately 80% of all sales occur between the second and fifth call.

However, the vast majority of salespeople quit after the first call. Only 20% of any sales force makes the third call…and that is when the majority of sales occur.

Rule 89
GET WIRED IN

Salespeople need to be in a zone where they can ignore outside distractions. Checking emails, talking to people in the office about the commute in that morning or thinking about what you want for lunch are all distractions that can affect your productivity.

A little chit chat here and there is healthy, but most of your day, you should be "wired in."

The movie "The Social Network" illustrates this anecdote perfectly. Sean Parker's character walks across the street to Zuckerburg's new California home office. He walks in and tries to introduce himself to a Facebooker who is writing code. The coder shakes his head and holds his hand up in denial, barely even acknowledging Parker. Zuckerburg then says, "Oh no, he is wired in."

ISLAND LORE

And that's what we are talking about! Get wired in and stay there. You must resist the temptation of talking to your really awesome co-workers too much. Especially in sales, where the cube mates tend to be super cool. (Did you see that game last night though?)

Sean Parker responds by saying: "That's what I'm talking about!"

Rule 90
OUTLAST YOUR SLUMP

Everyone has slumps. You will too.

The difference is that the most successful people stick around long enough to get out of them. It will be hard, but don't let things you can't control get the best of you.

There are many incredible stories of unimaginable slumps in sports, business, and plenty in sales, as well. Like Michael Jordan being cut from his high school basketball team, or Apple being crushed by Microsoft for what seemed like an eternity, or even the Curse of the Bambino for you baseball fans.

ISLAND LORE

Someone will win. Will it be you, or the slump?

All three of those slumps ended and yours will too.

Rule 91

ATTITUDE OF GRATITUDE

One of the healthiest emotions a human being can feel is gratitude. It's proven that people who genuinely feel thankful have less stress and live healthier, happier lives.

Why not apply the same attitude to your sales career? You will encounter many ebbs and flows in your career, and a lot of your success will depend on your ability to remain positive. Starting each day with a feeling of gratitude will give you excellent perspective and an advantage over the competition.

Gratitude comes with a certain amount of humbleness which is a very attractive quality.

Be confident, but be thankful at the same time. When you get discouraged, change your attitude to gratitude.

ISLAND LORE

Seriously, we could not be more thankful for the lives we are living; healthy families, friends and so many remarkable people to love. We think about these things every day. The Island is a thankful place.

Rule No. 91

You are now 91 Rules into The Pocket Guide For Sales Survival and have completed "Intermediate – Checking into Your Villa"

Before you become "Advanced" and an "Extended Island Vacationer"

Here is a story about…

The Attitude of Gratitude

MAKE GRATITUDE YOUR ATTITUDE
By Jason DeAmato

It is imperative in sales to always remain positive for one simple reason: It directly affects your success. If you are consistently feeling bad, you can expect your sales calls to also be consistently bad.

If you truly feel thankful every day, you will have no problem sustaining an outstanding attitude and being an elite salesperson.

The oldest of my three sisters, Janaelle, is two years younger than I am. We grew up very close and, thankfully, remain that way today.

Her husband, Brian, was diagnosed with brain cancer when he was 26 years old, before she met him. Brian, or as most people call him, "Humby," is a big guy standing about 6 feet tall and weighing over 200 pounds. He looks quite intimidating, but he is a big teddy bear.

"Humby" LOVES to use profanity, loves Seinfeld, football, being right, the beach, and cookies. He likes taking walks, loves coffee, he likes pizza and cussing. Wait, I already told you he likes to use profanity, which is OK, because you have to understand his true love for vulgarities for this story to really resonate.

Brian is an amazing dude. These quirks are just a small part of why we love him so dearly. We mostly love him for his huge heart and caring nature.

When he was first diagnosed at the age of 26, the doctors had no idea what his cancer was. For two weeks, as he waited for biopsy results, Brian didn't know if he had days, weeks, or months to live. One of the more scary times in his life, he was unsure of what to think, feel, and certainly had no idea how to act.

When the doctors came back, it was still unclear what type of cancer he had, but they knew it was a tumor in his brain. He was to start chemotherapy right away.

Brian began a long, arduous schedule of aggressive chemotherapy. He spent the next nine months doing chemotherapy, and, although his life would never be the same and it was a long and painful process for both him and his family, he made it out of treatment with a clean bill of health.

Brian met my sister, Janaelle, shortly after that experience.

They both were in love, and, like most people, excited about life and the future.

This all changed quickly.

Just six short months after Janaelle and Brian met, Brian experienced severe exhaustion. Because this came out of nowhere, he felt as though something was wrong, so he went in for some tests. The results of a biopsy were, again, the last thing anyone wanted to hear.

His cancer had returned.

The cancer was back less than three years later.

It was all happening again. Here he was, just 29 years of age, with his second round of brain cancer. Most people don't even have two rounds of back pain before age 29.

This second time around the diagnosis was clear: Central Nervous System Lymphoma. Sounds fun, huh? The last thing your central nervous system needs is something called lymphoma. I mean why couldn't it have been his pinky toe system? Or his back hair system?

For over **three and half years** (again) Brian was in and out of the hospital for chemotherapy. Brian and Janaelle looked around and saw everyone they knew living perfectly normal lives, engulfed in happiness while they felt like they were fighting for theirs on a daily basis.

There was no semblance of normality in their lives.
Most people go out to eat, they went to the hospital. Most make friends with the guy at the local coffee shop, they made friends with the resident nurses.

During treatment, Brian and Janaelle got engaged. It was an emotionally charged time, and they showed us that cancer would not stop their love and the plans they had for the future.

Soon after their engagement, and three and half years since his relapse, Brian was again declared cancer-free. Was this a miracle? Beating brain cancer … TWICE … before the age of 32. How is this possible?

They wed the following year.

Although as a couple they had taken some steps forward, Brian was still required to do chemotherapy every three months.

FOUR TIMES a year he was hooked up to an IV that streamed chemo into his veins faster than songs stream on iTunes.

Every three months, Brian and Janaelle would be reminded that his cancer had a 50% chance of returning.

They were being told that the chemo was working and to "just keep doing it," but they could not live like this. So they decided to seek a second opinion on their own. Upon visiting the Dana Farber Cancer Institute, they were delighted to learn that they actually do have options.

Make Gratitude Your Arttitude

Option one: live the rest of your life with chemotherapy and a 50% chance of cancer recurring.

Option two: a stem cell transplant which would reduce the chances of recurrence to 10%, but a stem cell transplant comes with extreme risk and sickness.

The answer was simple: stem cell transplant, and so the most challenging chapter begins.

Just Because I'm Losing Doesn't Mean I'm LOST…

A stem cell transplant requires extracting millions of healthy stem cells from the blood (that are too young to carry cancer) and freezing them. Then you basically send your immune system to the electric chair. They kill every cell and every trace of your immune system with extremely high doses of chemotherapy. Brian literally received about a year's worth of chemotherapy in eight days. Then, they infuse the healthy cells back into your blood. After the stem cell transplant is completed, it requires that Brian spend over a month in isolation in the hospital where visitors have to wear gloves and masks with limited visitation. If Brian so much as caught a cold, he could die. His immune system was so weak that even once released from the hospital, he was required to stay home in isolation for 100 days.

The Rock

Brian was a rock. Never too happy, never too sad, he kept his head on straight and saved his energy for fighting. The first time I saw Brian in the hospital during his stem cell transplant, it was same old Brian. It took about two minutes for him to make fun of me, saying the mask I was wearing (to contain germs) really improved my looks.

It took us about another 20 seconds to fall into our usual routine of letting everyone else in the room talk while we discuss the more important things in life: "Seinfeld" and "Curb Your Enthusiasm." We dove into trivia like it was a backyard barbecue. We ignored the fact that at this barbecue, it was his immune system that was getting grilled. He had tubes feeding him chemotherapy and pain medication, he'd lost weight, lost hair, lost a job, lost breakfast, lost dinner, lost lunch, lost drives to work, lost walking to Starbucks, lost freedom, lost time with his wife, lost time with family, lost any semblance of normalcy, lost, lost and lost.

But ... He never, even once, lost his positive attitude.

He knew he would beat this. He knew he would get out. And when he had every reason and excuse to sit and sulk, he sat in his hospital bed and said to me, "I'll give you five bucks if you can tell the names of the two NBC executives that Jerry and George pitch the pilot to."

Damn it! I only knew one ... Jay Crespi. I hate that he knows "Seinfeld" better than I do.

The Angel
Janaelle did everything for Brian. When Brian was released and required to be in isolation for 100 days at home, she took care of everything. Their apartment needed to be disinfected every single day, she paid the bills, ran the errands, prepared special meals daily and took on all financial responsibilities. There was no time for working on a relationship, or enjoying their marriage. There was no going out to eat, to the movies or to see friends.

Their lives revolved around Brian getting better. Even though he technically had no cancer in his body, he was his sickest and weakest yet, and required her attention more than ever. Their normal lives had been electro shocked out of coherence and all we could do was pray there was enough positive voltage in the universe to electro shock them back. Janaelle's positive attitude was a mandatory entity. Similar to how your sales cube mate's attitude affects your attitude, Brian needed Janaelle to be positive.

Big Fish in a Little Pond...
The stem cell transplant was successful. Brian no longer needs chemo-

Make Gratitude Your Arttitude

therapy and he's been cancer free for over two years. We now celebrate his new birthday, which is January 15th, the day he had millions of cancer-free stem cells infused back into his body. They had a saying in the hospital and even made T-shirts when they got home that read "LISTC."

LISTC = Love Is Stronger Than Cancer
You may think that stories about love and thankfulness helping to beat cancer do not belong in a sales book.

But they do.

If you fill your life with love and gratitude, which are two of the most powerful and positive emotions, you will live a good life and you will be excellent within your talents.

Brian has taken the lessons he learned from his battle and used them to build a successful **sales** career, and he knows that his attitude is the key to his success.

I do believe that we control our own attitudes, and even in the toughest of times you can focus on the little victories. You must **believe** you are going to succeed.

One early August afternoon, Brian and I sat waist deep in the beautiful Atlantic Ocean. It was truly one of those perfect summer days. Nothing was planned other than the beach, beers and bocce ball.

After a long conversation where we discussed his entire ordeal with cancer and the rawest of emotions he experienced, I asked him, "How did you make it through all of that, what do you think helped you survive?"

He looked at me and said, "Through everything, I just kept the thought in my head that everything happens for a reason. That allowed me to focus on one thing at a time and be grateful for what I had, and in the end remain positive."

I couldn't believe that someone with such a terrible hand dealt to him would tell me that he felt "everything happened for a reason." Even though I knew he truly felt this way, I was still so blown away by the guts he had.

Even though I was pretty sure I knew the answer, I had to ask him.

"Do you think that staying positive was the key to beating this?"

Humby responded with two words: "Absofuckinlutely, kid."

Brian's story is proof that an attitude of gratitude is one of the most powerful emotions human beings can have and will impact your success.

Before cancer, Brian had a job in finance. Now he works in sales. Surprised?

He attributes his success in sales to his ability to stay thankful and positive.

You may spend one year, two years, or 20 years in sales. During those years you will encounter many ebbs and flows. The key to your success will depend upon how you handle those ebbs and flows. Start tapping into why you are grateful and watch the results.

You do not need to beat cancer to be thankful and have a great attitude in sales, but it doesn't hurt either.

Make gratitude your attitude!

-Jason DeAmato

Advanced

EXTENDED ISLAND VACATIONER

DIG INTO QUESTIONS

Two customers ask the same question: How much does your product cost?

Your knee-jerk response is probably to answer their question with a dollar amount. But hold on a second ... Let's think about this.

Do you even know if they're both asking the question for the same reason? What if one wants the most affordable price, while the other wants to spend top dollar for a top product because the last time they bought a cheap one, they weren't happy?

The only way you can know for sure is by turning the conversation around and asking them. "That's a great question! Why do you ask?" Try it. You'll be surprised at the answers you get—and even more surprised by how helpful the information is.

You may think asking questions is enough. But dig into the motivations behind those questions. Now you're really getting useful information. Dig it?

ISLAND LORE

Try using the pain funnel, which was coined by the late David Sandler. Can you tell me more about that? How long has this been a problem? What have you tried to do about it? How much do you suppose that has cost you? How do you feel about that? What happens if you do nothing?

Rule 93
MIRROR YOUR CUSTOMER

Some customers want facts. Some want attention. Some want to be heard, and some want to listen.

Mirror your customer's personality, tone and cadence. Evaluate their personality and adjust.

Know what type of person you are in a relationship with and give them the style of communication they need. It's so crucial to know who your customer is and what makes them tick.

ISLAND LORE

People buy things from people they like. When you mirror your customer, your likability skyrockets.

People love to talk about themselves, so make sure you are asking questions about who they are. More importantly, listen to their answers.

Rule No. 93

CARE ABOUT EACH SECOND (TICK...TICK...TICK)

No matter where you work as a salesperson, you do not have the liberty of taking a day off. You read that right. In fact, you can't even take a second off.

You need to care about every single second you exist.

If you care about everything you do, you will be forced to improve your results.

As an example, don't just write your goals down when your boss asks you to, you should have goals because YOU want to....and don't just turn your attitude on when the customer picks up the phone... Attitude should be on all day long... every......second! Even when no one is watching.

ISLAND LORE

People who live on the Island of Sales care about everything. The ones who don't care eventually get eaten by the birds. (Ouch!) And it's a slow, painful death. So you better care about this second ... and this one ... and this one. Good job.
Shoo, birds! Shoo!

Rule 95
ASK FOR THE SALE

For some reason, some people are afraid to ask for the sale. Our advice to those who are afraid is simple: Get over it!

When it comes to breaking down this barrier, it's all about jumping in the water. The first time you asked someone for a date, it wasn't easy, but the more you do it, the easier it becomes.

By the way, IT'S OK!

It's completely normal to be afraid of this. It's one of the most common types of sales reluctance found in salespeople. However, it doesn't mean its ok not to recognize and change it.

The more confident you become asking for the sale, the easier and more EFFECTIVE it becomes.

People who are great at asking for business come off as confident and businesslike. If a customer feels you are afraid to ask for business, they will also feel there is a reason you are afraid. Like maybe your product or service is not worth it.

ISLAND LORE

On the Island, we are very clear and confident about asking for business. Observe: **"If you think this book helped you, please buy two more to give as gifts. It's no secret we make money off of book sales. We like money. But we love helping people improve the most."** See how easy that was?

Rule No. 95

Rule 96

GET EDUCATED

Understand the value in furthering
your educational background.
Maybe a BA, BS, MBA or PhD is
for you; they rarely hurt.

The key is not only finding the right
path, but finding a subject you will
love learning about.

Always consider furthering your
formal education.

ISLAND LORE

As far as our educations
go, we don't like to brag,
but … We can read—and
pretty fast, too!

Without college, we would have no idea what a flow chart is … and you
never know when you're going to need to make a flow chart on the go!

Companies in the United States spend $7.1 Billion annually on Sales Training.

This makes us feel really good about charging less than the cost of a couple drinks at the bar for the most crucial sales training book every team needs!

The Pocket Guide For Sales Survival!

Fact No. 4

Rule 97

BUILD (THE CORRECT) EXPECTATIONS

Setting proper expectations is one of the most important things you can do in business.

Tell your customer what to expect of you. And tell them what you expect of them.

Setting clear expectations from the beginning is key to a smooth and honest relationship.

ISLAND LORE

You always know what to expect on the Island. For example, you can expect to get better as a sales professional. And you can always expect a healthy dose of mediocre jokes.

Don't be afraid to explain the cold, hard facts, even if they can be portrayed as less than positive. ALWAYS set the correct expectations!

This is a good rule to read at least five times a day.

Rule 98

EDUCATE TODAY ... SELL TOMORROW

You don't always have to get commitment on the first meeting.

In fact, if you feel like "going for it" will be too aggressive, the best thing to do is hold off. Instead, focus on educating and defining needs.

ISLAND LORE

Let each unique situation dictate when you close.

Some customers will need time to think over everything they've learned.

Give them time. It's OK to sell tomorrow in these situations.

Plus, it gives you more time to build a relationship.

Rule No. 98

RECAP THE LITTLE THINGS, TOO

Recap and repeat when necessary. People almost never remember everything you say.

A quick recap can be the difference between information sticking or being lost FOREVER.

Of course, recapping at the end of every presentation is imperative, but also recap certain points of conversations.

If you recap six times, your prospect is six times more likely to remember what you said.

ISLAND LORE

Recap and repeat when necessary. People never remember everything you say. A quick recap can be the difference in information sticking or being lost FOREVER. Of course recapping at the end of every presentation is imperative, but also recap certain points of conversations. If you recap six times, your prospect is six times more likely to remember what you said.

Any of this sound familiar ... Or do you need ANOTHER recap?

MAKE IT EASY FOR PEOPLE

One of the most important things you can do is to make your customer's life easy.

Try to think one step ahead of every person you deal with and always give them the path of least resistance.

We're not saying lay down and be a doormat—just make interactions flow with ease. The less complicated your relationships are, the more people will like to deal with you.

ISLAND LORE

For your first trip to The Island of Sales, we will pick you up at your desired time and location. Nothing but limos, yachts and private jets baby!

Rule No. 100

Rule 101
NEVER ENTER COMBAT

Your prospects should always be
walking with you through a process.

Never alienate your client or make
them feel like they are alone.

Consultants never use combative
language or behavior.

ISLAND LORE

As you probably guessed,
we're lovers, not fighters,
on the Island.

If a customer wants to engage you in a fight, suggest that they take up
mixed martial arts and move on.

Rule 102
GO FOR THE NO!

Don't be afraid to go for a no.

"My biggest fear is that we leave each other, both enthusiastic about this deal, but then work catches up to us and we end up missing each other or chasing each other around and playing phone tag."

"If we don't have a match, will you feel comfortable telling me 'no'? Great, because a valid fear is that you are no longer interested but don't want to let me down. And I end up pestering you with calls and emails when really you decided to go in a different direction. You won't hurt my feelings saying 'no,' as long as you tell me why."

Believe it or not, the more you hear "no" the more you will hear "yes." This may not seem to make much sense now, but trust us: GO FOR THE "NO"!

ISLAND LORE

On the Island we love when people say 'no.' At least we got an honest answer. Maybe we work through it and maybe we don't. At least we have healthy communication.

Rule 103

SPEAK NOW OR FOREVER HOLD YOUR PEACE!

"I think I need some time to think this over"

The next time your prospect tells you they want to think about it, just say this:

"In my experience, a lot of times when someone says they want to think about it, they really are just trying not to hurt my feelings.

"For instance, if I asked the woman of my dreams if she would marry me and she said she wanted to think about it ... Probably not good for me, right?

ISLAND LORE

If the woman of your dreams says she wants to think about it, she just became the woman of your nightmares. Either way, you better wake up!

"Don't worry, I can handle it if you say no, just tell me now, and again I am ok with hearing any of your apprehensions, you won't hurt my feelings."

Rule 104

SEEK OUT MENTORS

Having great mentors will change the entire scope of your career. But you shouldn't wait around for them to appear. Instead, take control and seek them out.

You may have many different mentors over the course of your life and career. Different people will influence you in different ways, but make no mistake: they will change your life for the better.

Anyone who's enjoyed success has had someone in their life who provided guidance. We are all so lucky to have these people in our lives.

ISLAND LORE

Looking for a mentor? You've come to the right place! The Island was built on outstanding mentorship. It took a small army, but thank you to everyone who helped us two misfits!

Rule 105

RECOGNIZE THE HEIGHT OF IMPULSE

There are two big mistakes you can make as a salesperson: closing too early and closing too late.

The Height of Impulse is the period of time in the sales process where the client is most likely to commit to you. It can last one minute, five minutes, five days or even a month, but every sale has one. It can occur during the first few minutes of the first conversation, or it can come at the end of the sales cycle, days, weeks or months later. Or it could be anywhere in between.

ISLAND LORE

The Island doesn't like it when you miss buying signs. If you wear out your welcome with random precision, you are better off as a painter, piper or prisoner.

The key is for the salesperson to always be watching for the Height of Impulse and then to CLOSE when it strikes. Most salespeople innately know when to close. But when you're dealing with more subtle clients, you must watch for buying signs and close when the impulse is highest.

In longer sales cycles where there are multiple commitment moments, you will have multiple Height of Impulse points. Handle with care, as long sales cycles carry larger risk. Watch for the Height of Impulse when it pertains to moving the sale forward. Get little pieces of commitment and stay focused on each segment. Sooner, rather than later, the process will be complete.

Rule 106

ASSUME THE SALE AND CLOSE WITH CONFIDENCE

The reason there is empty space at the beginning of this book is specifically for you to help others.

Go out and buy a few copies of this book, personalize each copy in that empty space with a nice message to someone you know who is also on The Island of Sales, and give them this "Pocket Guide for Sales Survival" so that they may benefit from the timeless wisdom contained within.

ISLAND LORE

We think we made our point here: Close with shameless confidence! www.thebestsalesbook.com

You know people who will benefit from reading this book. In fact, you know more than one.

There's no better way to tell someone you care than by giving them a book, personalized from you, that will help them increase their paycheck and dramatically advance their career growth.

Rule No. 106

Rule 107
OUTLINE YOUR AGENDA

Think about the countless presentations you've had to sit through in your life. Which type do you prefer: the ones where the speaker launches in without giving you any indication of where they're going, or the ones where the speaker maps out their agenda before they begin?

Good presenters always provide the audience an outline before they begin. The best presenters outline before they begin and again before each segment.

And yet, most salespeople don't bother to outline their presentations to customers.

The goal of outlining a call is to let your prospect know exactly what you plan to cover in your time with them. Outlining your call allows you to:

• Set the expectation and put your customer at ease
  • Gain control of the call
  • Easily transition to each step of the process
  • Increase chances of closing

That last bullet point is really all the motivation you should need!

ISLAND LORE

Welcome to The Island of Sales. Your first day on the Island will include some early morning rum-infused smoothies, followed by an afternoon lunch and nap. And following tonight's dinner there will be more rum and a bonfire visible from space! Does that make sense?

Rule No. 107

Island of Sales

Rule 108

BUILD IMPULSE

It's one thing to recognize the Height of Impulse, but it all starts with building that impulse early. People will procrastinate by nature, so you need to expose and leverage the reasons to buy.

It may be with value propositions or sense of urgency, but from the beginning of your relationship, you need to build impulse.

ISLAND LORE

With each bit of Island lore you read, you are feeling more and more like you would like to actually visit The Island of Sales. With cool people, lots of things to learn, great networking … well … the impulse is building. We are going to wait until the Height of Impulse to tell you where the Island is. Don't worry— it doesn't involve an Oceanic flight from Sydney to LAX … or a malaria shot.

Rule No. 108

JUST CLOSE IT

"Every morning in Africa, a gazelle wakes up. It knows it must run faster than the fastest lion or it will be killed. Every morning a lion wakes up. It knows it must outrun the slowest gazelle or it will starve to death. It doesn't matter whether you are a lion or a gazelle... when the sun comes up; you'd better be running..." – Christopher McDougall

> ## ISLAND LORE
>
> Close every opportunity. It doesn't matter if it's "yes" or "no." Just close it.

Every morning on The Island of Sales, a prospect wakes up...

When it comes to closing, sometimes you should close early, sometimes you should close late, sometimes you should close hard, and sometimes you should close soft. One thing is for sure: When the sun comes up, you'd better be closing!

Rule 110
TEACH WHAT YOU LEARN

What's the old saying? "Those who can, do. Those who can't, teach."

Well, on The Island of Sales, we'd like to amend that: "Those who can, do. Those who can and want to get better, teach."

The best way to learn something is to teach it.

You know a lot about sales. You know a lot about your product. You have the ability to convey it clearly to others. Teach it!

The takeaway is remarkable. You will learn your craft better by teaching it to others.

ISLAND LORE

One of the motivations for writing this book is pure selfishness: We truly believe it will help us on a daily basis in our own sales careers. We wanted an all-encompassing guide. Every moment we spend teaching, we are encouraging ourselves to apply the same lessons.

Rule 111
BE CREDIBLE

What's your "credit score" in sales? Do you always deliver? Are you always on time? Do you always send the follow-up information you promised during the call?

Not only do your customers evaluate this, but so does your boss. Have impeccable "credit" when it comes to your word.

It's rare to find people you can truly count on. Be one of those people. Boost your sales credit score and benefit from the results!

Students who graduated from a sales program "ramp up" 50% faster and are 30% less likely to turn over than those who don't!

So why do only 150 out of the 4000 Universities in the United States have sales programs?

Rule 112

HELP OTHERS HIT THEIR GOALS

When is the last time you asked a prospect, a friend, someone you manage, or someone you care about what their goals are?

Try it. Ask someone what their goals are and then try your best to help that person reach those goals.

When it comes to people on your team, there is no question that if you help enough people hit their goals, you will certainly be far more likely to hit yours!

ISLAND LORE

Being No. 1 is great, but helping someone else become No. 1 is even better. You can have both.

Selflessness is a very attractive quality, and true leaders usually have it in spades.

Rule 113

FIND YOUR INSPIRATION

Life won't always provide you
the necessary motivation to keep
moving forward. Nor will your job.

Whatever it is, whatever it takes,
whatever you need, find that
inspiration and apply it.

And you may have several sources
of inspiration; never stop seeking
additional inspirational avenues.

ISLAND LORE

We're so inspired, we built
an island. It's an imaginary
one, granted, but hey,
that took some seriously
imaginative inspiration!

Maybe your inspiration is helping others. Maybe it's providing for your
family's future. Or maybe it's your desire to prove to the world that you
can succeed—in spite of the hand you've been dealt.

Staying consistently inspired throughout your career is crucial to
long-term success. You have complete control over this. An uninspired
salesman is like a dog with no appetite.

Your business has no purpose if you are not inspired.

Rule No. 113

Rule 114

GO WITH YOUR GUT

Many of the decisions you will face in your sales career require immediate action and the ability to quickly measure risk versus reward. The best tool you have to handle these situations are your instincts.

Like animals in the wild, every person has their own set of instincts (remember "fight vs. flight" from biology class?). Everyone has instincts, it's just that some people trust in them more than others. But we all have them. Use them!

If you're deeply instinctive and the decisions you make when you "listen to your gut" always work out, stick with it!

ISLAND LORE

The only time we don't trust our gut is when it's telling us to quit ... or to put anchovies on our pizza.

If you're less convinced that your "gut feelings" are usually accurate, then follow these instincts. They're saying you may need to take fewer chances, use more logic and play it safe.

Rule 115

LEVERAGE YOUR INTELLIGENCE

Work smarter, not harder.

Gather intelligence, use intelligence, and be intelligent.

Use good judgment, use your smarts, and make good decisions.

Not thinking things through and making careless moves will certainly stunt the growth of your sales career.

ISLAND LORE

"We all know that light travels faster than sound. That's why certain people appear bright until you hear them speak."
– Albert Einstein

For example, don't just call or email one of your prospects simply for the sake of reaching out to them, especially when you have nothing of value to share. Think about what exactly you can do or say to drive the deal forward aside from just "checking in."

Slow down and always think things through twice before action.

Think twice. Act once.

Rule 116

UNDERSTAND AND UTILIZE TEAMWORK

Imagine a football team that fielded 11 quarterbacks on offense at the same time.

Even if each one were an All-Pro, it would be a terrible offense. For starters, they'd all be yelling over each other trying to call the play.

On any team, there are different people with different positions. Some block, some tackle. Some run, some catch. Some throw, some kick.

ISLAND LORE

"Talent wins games, but teamwork and intelligence win championships." – Michael Jordan

Use your team to your advantage. Behind every successful sales professional is a great support structure—not just in the immediate department, but also throughout the company.

Leverage the people on your team; no one can survive on the Island alone.

Rule 117

SEEK CONSTRUCTIVE CRITICISM

It's tough for most people to hear what their peers, colleagues or mentors have to say about their weaknesses. It can be a very humbling process, but it's an undertaking that you must begin immediately.

Ask for constructive criticism as often as you can.

Seeking out weaknesses is not something most people do often, but we should. Be different. It's a tough pill to swallow, but you will benefit in the long run.

It is very important not take constructive feedback personally; you should simply focus on the behavior and the results.

Think of perfecting yourself and your sales abilities the same way that a golfer perfects his or her golf swing.

ISLAND LORE

You are reading this book because you care about your career. Take the next step and ask someone close to you for some constructive feedback. The sooner you can start making improvements, the sooner your closing percentage goes up.

Just think about how much further you will go when you perfect that swing and make improvements you may not even have been aware that you needed to make.

Rule 118

B3

This is a rule with three parts!

Be Yourself
Be Loved
Be Remembered

Be Yourself

Although it's important to adapt to various situations and the different personalities of clients, you must always remain true to yourself.

The best salespeople on the planet have core values and characteristics that always stay true. Those same people are also able to adapt to many different situations, such as different cultures, personalities, economic climates, intellects, and atmospheres.

The ability to be yourself and yet adapt to other variables in real time is one of the most coveted characteristics in salespeople.

ISLAND LORE

No posers allowed on the Island.

Be Loved

All things being equal, people buy from people they like. For instance, say you have a daughter. If your daughter is selling a box of Girl Scout cookies for $10 and your neighbor's daughter is selling that same box of Girl Scout cookies for $10, you're going to buy them from your daughter.

Now, what if your daughter's box of Girl Scout cookies was $10 but the neighbor's daughter had them for $7?

We bet a box of Thin Mints that you'd STILL buy them from your own daughter because even when things are unequal, people STILL buy from people they like!

Salespeople need to be likable. We want you to bring it to the next level. Be Loved.

Enough said.

ISLAND LORE

We eat lots of cookies.

Rule No. 118

(Rule 118 continued)

Be Remembered

You never want to be on a sales call where you are just as liked as the competition, but not as memorable.

People usually remember personal things about each other. This is humanistic selling at its best.

Remember your client's children and your client will remember you.

Important note to Rule #118 B3: In the rare occasion you are not liked, it is better to be forgotten. Maybe you can try again next year!

ISLAND LORE

Who is this again? Oh, sorry, not interested.

Rule 119
PAY ATTENTION TO DETAIL

Every salesperson needs to be reminded to pay attention to detail, at least once a week.

Is your client's son named Luke or Duke? Memorizing this could be the difference between closing and coming up empty.

Names, dates, times, prices, promises and product knowledge are all like that carton of milk you promised to pick up on the way home—you better remember them.

Pay attention to detail!

In all seriousness, don't' forget ...
"The Devil is in the details."

Rule 120

NO ALARMS AND NO SURPRISES

Don't surprise your customers. It may cost you the sale you worked so hard on.

Catching your customer off guard with unexpected hurdles, costs or requirements can impede business in a big way.

Set clear expectations and stick to the plan.

Keep your customers in the light; you will see stacks of repeat business and referrals if you reduce surprises at all costs.

ISLAND LORE

On those very rare occasions where you can surprise your client, it absolutely must be something positive that will drive the sales process forward, not put on the brakes!

Rule 121
PRESENT THE PRICE

Customer: "How much does that cost?"
You: "Six million dollars!"
Customer: "Wow, that is a great price!"
You: "I know, right! Would you like two?"
Customer: "Yes, please!"

How likely is that to happen?

Make sure to have a presentation for price. Always try to build value before mentioning price when you can.

Practice how you present price. This is where a lot of salespeople could use improvement.

Your customer needs to think about and understand the value of your product. If you blurt out a price without building value, it can cheapen your product.

When it does come time to mention numbers, make sure you are Calm, Confident, and Candid. The three C's.

Sometimes your prospect will want price right away, even before you have had the chance to build value. We have all been there. You would love to slow the conversation down, but the prospect is demanding a ballpark number.

This is ok ... but remember ... Deliver the price with the 3 C's, and then make an attempt to build value and justify costs if necessary.

Calm – Confident - Candid

Rule No. 121

Rule 122
ASK YES-YES QUESTIONS

When possible, create a winning scenario for your prospect by asking yes-yes questions.

Understanding someone's needs is crucial in this situation.

Remember to provide winning options. When people are given fewer choices, it makes their decision process much easier.

ISLAND LORE

The Island's asks: Would you like to make more money or get promoted?

Would you like to sign up now or come back in 10 minutes?

Would you like two widgets today or only one?

Rule 123

SILENCE IS SPLENDID

We could all use a little more silence in our lives. So why are we so afraid of it when it comes to selling?

Dominant salespeople are usually extremely comfortable with silence.

Ask a question ... silence.

Make an open-ended statement ... silence.

Ask for commitment ... silence.

ISLAND LORE

When selling, especially immediately after closing, the first one to speak always loses. Silence Earthling!

Let people talk. You will extract piles of useful data this way.

Use silence to your advantage.

It will transform you into the confident closer you know is inside of you!

Rule 124

THERE'S MORE TO IT, THAN JUST CLOSING

If the only thing you have in mind is to actualize a sale, then that's the only thing you'll be really effective at.

There's so much more to sales than just getting someone to sign on the dotted line.

Take the time and make the effort to maximize the potential of every customer. After all, you may not be talking to just any customer; you may be talking to a referral who can lead you to 20 more customers.

ISLAND LORE

Become comfortable with the subtleties of how and when to close. The Island is watching and listening closely.

You also want to make sure you bring quality customers in the door. Rushing someone to sign will bring customers that cancel. Take your time and be aware that it's not always about closing.

Rule 125

BE RESILIENT

Facing adversity is a good thing. Like a bag of tea, you'll never know how strong you are until you're in hot water.

Everyone finds themselves in some hot water during their sales career, and you're no different. You're bound to encounter some tough times and low points, so grow some thick skin!

Get ready for the rejection. Be prepared for the ebbs. Dig deep and be more resilient than the next person.

ISLAND LORE

The Island sits right in the hurricane belt, and we like it that way. The more storms we withstand, the harder it is to take us down. Every year the Island gets tougher!

Your career will certainly have many sprints (that's the nature of sales), but, in the end, your career is a marathon. Don't panic and overreact to things that are happening now. Be strong and stay focused on the long-distance run.

Rule No. 125

Rule 126

WORK SMART – BE EFFICIENT

Don't waste time. Find out the quickest way to get things done and then execute.

Are you on Facebook, Twitter or ESPN.com during your workday?

Waste of time.

Get serious and ditch all non-productive behaviors.

The more experienced you get, the better you will become at getting things done more efficiently. If the opposite is happening, you may want to investigate what is contributing to your long, inefficient hours.

ISLAND LORE

Using social media and surfing the web to facilitate business, generate leads or research your prospects is one thing … stalking your ex and tweeting about your Friday night plans is something the Island calls "slacking."

Over 50% of sales managers are too busy to train and develop their sales teams.

Rule 127

DRINK MENTAL MARTINIS

Learn how to take breaks and step away when you need to. Have a mental martini.

A healthy attitude is your most important sales weapon, so you have to catch yourself when you feel like you need a break.

We've asked thousands of people what they do when they're having a bad day. Their answers include:
• Listen to music
• Do some yoga
• Call a friend
• Get a little exercise
• Go for a walk
• Talk to someone funny
• Wear a bright color
• Eat some candy

ISLAND LORE

Whatever your mental martini is, consider this your prescription to drink as many as you need a day. We can hear it now: "Hey, you're that idiot author who convinced my top salesperson to call a friend 37 times a day!"

Rule No. 127

Rule 128
ADAPT TO YOUR CUSTOMERS

Adapting to your customer is all about putting yourself on the same page.

If your customer is a 30-something truck driver from Maine, you need to be on the same page as he is. If your customer is a retired, divorced mother of three from Boca Raton, you need to be on the same page as she is.

This specifically means adapting to things like tone, pace of speaking, formal or informal language, eye contact, intellect, body language, and vocabulary.

This not only makes your prospect more comfortable, but it will make you more comfortable, as well.

ISLAND LORE

Why couldn't there be some place, some happy place, like an island, for example, where everyone is so easy to talk to?

The quicker you adapt to a customer's personality style, the quicker you can start the sales process. The better you adapt, the better your chances of getting the sale.

Rule 129

PROGRESSION OVER PERFECTION

Measure your success by how far you have come in relation to where you started.

Before you measure yourself against others, measure this week's YOU vs. last week's YOU.

Progression comes first.

Perfection comes later.

ISLAND LORE

Perfection in sales is like perfection in parenting. It will never happen. Although, you should always strive for it. The best practice for this is focusing on your progress. Now go eat your vegetables!

Rule No. 129

You are about to become an "Expert" or "An Island Resident!"

Before you embark on the last 31 Rules in

The Pocket Guide For Sales Survival...

Let us share a quick story,

Just to make sure you are

LISTENING

Two Ears and One Mouth

TWO EARS AND ONE MOUTH
By Randy Bernard

My grandfather was a brilliant guy, and he was always teaching me lessons.

When I was a teenager, he often had interesting riddles for me that would keep me guessing for hours.

As I became a young adult, before my grandfather passed, he would ask me really out of the box, thought provoking questions that always made me stop in my tracks. He would ask me why I made certain decisions, or why I chose the friends I chose, or why I picked the College I picked, or the job, or the girl … and so forth and so on.

The older my grandfather got, the less involved and mysterious his teachings became, until the point where the majority of time we spent together towards the end was simply spent as a transfer of knowledge. He would just tell me the things he wanted me to know.

"Randy, the way you choose to spend the 4 years you will be in college will have a huge impact on the next 40 years of your life."

"Randy, Integrity is something that cannot be purchased, it cannot be sold, but it can be lost little by little, one broken promise at a time."

"Randy, to become a millionaire all you have to do is have one million one dollar bills. Every time you get a one dollar bill, don't give it to anyone else. How many do you have now?"

"Randy, when you are out to breakfast at a restaurant, don't EVER order orange juice! It comes in that tiny little cup and costs more than an entire carton at the store!"

Of course, each piece of advice has had varying degrees of importance …

The best piece of advice he ever gave me that really related to sales was when he told me that I had **two ears and only one mouth.**

About 6 months after my grandfather passed away I was in California working at my first sales job ever, going door to door selling office supplies.

My job was to walk into offices completely cold, no appointment, with a big thick Staples catalog and try to sell them office supplies. Yep, office supplies. We are talking post-it notes, reams of paper, push pins, paper clips and pens.

Don't get me wrong, I had photocopiers and printers on the inside back cover of my catalog, but those were only for the elite sales veterans at our company. I was only 3 months in, so we are talking 3 ring binders and Scotch tape here.

One day, I was walking down Ventura Boulevard, knocking on doors and attempting to sell people office supplies. If you have ever sold the same thing for a long time or had to pitch 100 different people in one day with the same identical pitch, you know that you can start to just "go through the motions" if you aren't careful.

Although it was 11 years and probably 100,000 sales pitches ago, I remember this particular door like it was yesterday. I stormed into this office, and right there in front of me was a woman standing behind the desk with an exceptionally welcoming look on her face.

Typically, I would get asked to leave or even kicked out of most offices. To my surprise, the woman stood with a smile on her face and did not kick me out of her office, so I gathered my nerves and started to pitch.

Our eyes locked and I started in. "Hi, How are you? My name is Randy, I am with Staples office supplies. The reason I am out here today is because we are running a huge promotion here in your area and ..."

I went on and delivered the pitch of a lifetime. We are talking about the type of sales pitch that would make Anthony Robbins jealous. Zig Ziglar would want to know me and shake my hand out of respect ... type of pitch ... this thing was EPIC.

At about the 4 or 5 minute mark I paused and she was in awe. No yelling, no pointing, I mean she was INTO IT!

I went on for about another 5 minutes. I was just weaving the English language like a Sales Ninja! I was delivering a sales pitch which measured up with the caliber of the Mona Lisa. I droned on about discounted prices and free gifts. I whipped out phrases like "today only" and "earn your business" and this woman was EATING-IT-UP.

I could see it in her eyes. She was agreeing and smiling at every turn. When I mentioned "free delivery" or "net 30 billing" her eyes lit up. When I flipped through pages and pointed at products, the edges of her mouth curled up in a grin. As I pointed at specialty items and ink cartridges, her eyes squinted and she nodded in agreement ... I absolutely KNEW I had a sale.

As my sales pitch came to an end and my confidence level peaked through the clouds, I mustered up the courage to ask the most terrifying, important question, a sales guy could ever ask, but today ... I already knew the answer.

I was already cashing the check.

Almost as if in slow motion, I leaned against the desk, cocked my head to the side and delivered my line:

"So" I said, "How many can I get you today, do you want to get 3 of them, or just go with the 1?"

The woman lifted her heels off of the ground, stood on her tippy toes, and that ever present smile that had existed since the moment I walked in the door almost 10 minutes earlier, widened even more to the point where she looked as if she just won the lottery.

She clasped her hands and picked up the catalog and my heart skipped a beat. She was going to say the most sought after words a sales guy at my company could ever hear. She was flipping to the back page, and she wanted a copier. I could smell it. I could FEEL it, I could hear those sweet words just rolling off her tongue.

She opened her mouth ... and out spilled the most enlightening three words I had ever heard in my life ...

She said .... "NO SPEAKA ENGLISH."

I reached for the catalogue, as she politely handed it towards me, and I slid it into my bag. I smiled and nodded, said thank you, turned and walked out of the office. Many thoughts were racing through my head and different emotions were swarming in my belly, but all I could think about was my grandfather.

About 6 months earlier I was having a conversation with my grandfather, which I later found out was one of the last conversations I would ever have with him, and he pulled me in close and he said to me:

"Randy, you have two ears and only one mouth. You should always listen, twice as much as you speak."

It was only then, as I walked down Ventura Boulevard, completely discouraged, that I realized why my grandfather was so brilliant. I figured out how he amassed such a huge amount of knowledge and facts, lessons and answers, guidance and truth.

It was because he listened.

I don't think there is a more important skill that a sales person can master than listening to their customers. If you simply stop talking and start listening, your customers will tell you everything you need to know to close the sale.

Asking questions and listening to the answers is how elite, professional sales people win.

Listen to your customers, rather than just waiting for them to stop talking. I encourage you to hear what they are saying, rather than just preparing for what you are about to say next. I want you to listen not only to what they say, but how they say it, and I promise you that you will advance in your sales career exponentially.

Don't be too busy selling to actually hear what your customers have to say, you might find out that they don't even speak the language.

My grandfather taught me many lessons. I appreciated them all and I definitely heard him tell me that I should always have two ears and only one mouth ...

... but I didn't listen.

-Randy Bernard

Two Ears and One Mouth

Expert

ISLAND
RESIDENT

Rule 130

DON'T GIVE AWAY THE GOODS TOO SOON

Before you divulge important information such as price points, obligations, and terms of a contract, make sure you have built value.

If I have a car hidden behind a door and tell you I will sell it to you for $200,000, what would you say?

Two-hundred grand is a lot of money. What if it's a broken-down Volkswagen? But what if it's a $4 million dollar Bentley?

ISLAND LORE

Don't jump the gun, because you almost got a 4 million dollar car for $200k.

The point is, too much information too soon can hurt you. Customers may ask about price, contracts and other obligations before they see the value.

So, you must start building value early.

Build value the right way, and they will give you all the buying signs you need.

Rule 131

TAKE YOUR PROSPECT'S TEMPERATURE

Taking your prospect's temperature is an attempt to gauge your customer's interest level. It's NOT an attempt to close the deal. There's a big difference, and it's crucial to understand the difference. A close asks for commitment, while a Temperature Close asks for an OPINION.

For example, ask your prospect a question, and offer some options for them to choose from.

"John, in your opinion, what do you see as the most attractive aspect of our product?

• Our 90-day money-back guarantee?
• The 97% customer approval rating?
• Our very competitive pricing?"

Once you have posed this question you will get one of two possible outcomes. They will:
• Answer with one of the examples you gave.
• Waiver and not be able to answer.

If they answer, you can now gauge their excitement and commitment level through tone and how serious they sound about one of your benefits. If they sound very interested, this is also a very nice approach to ease into a close.

If they are unable to provide a clear or convincing answer, they either were not listening, or they may not be interested. Either way, now it's time to ask them again and make sure the problem is not YOU. If they fail the second Temperature Close, it's now time to ask them if you are on the same page.

Taking your prospect's temperature is to be used with clients who are very hard to read. You don't want to use this on someone who has clearly defined their needs and interest level.

ISLAND LORE

On the Island, we take all of our cold prospects and throw them on the grill. Nice and easy!

Rule 132
ENJOY WORK/LIFE BALANCE

They say when you do what you love; you never work another day in your life.

Since you spend most of your life working, you have to enjoy your work.

Enjoying life is crucial to having a good balance. Just like with a car, if you do nothing but grind it out and push too hard, sooner or later you damage the engine parts.

Balance your life with hard work, rest and enjoyment. You can find the perfect formula for optimal performance and it always contains a good amount of both work and play.

ISLAND LORE

On the Island we work extremely hard, but we also kick it into neutral and know how to chillax like there's no tomorrow. Yup … chillax.

Compartmentalize. If you're a salesperson, you most likely carry a smartphone that is always connecting you back to the job. Shut it off sometimes. You must compartmentalize and leave work at work. When you're home, be home.

Rule No. 132

Rule 133

ALWAYS MOVE TOWARD A CLOSE

Does always moving toward a close mean you're always asking for the business? No. Instead, you're always doing things that make it more likely for you to close.

This could mean building a relationship, creating urgency or talking about the next step. Anything that increases your chances of commitment.

Over time, you will learn how to make every word, every question, count. This rule is something you will "feel" if you are in tune to your sales process.

ISLAND LORE

Top salespeople very rarely waste time or words. Each conversation that takes place with a customer should be designed to drive the sale forward, moving you towards the close.

If everything you do moves you closer to commitment, you're on the right track. Some salespeople do this naturally. Others need to develop this skill over time.

Rule 134
BE INNOVATIVE

Get creative, try new things and don't be afraid to innovate. Practice critical thinking and attack your sales pipeline from different angles.

If you think, you will be innovating.

Do not just toe the line at work. Dare to be different.

If you can be a problem-solver, not a problem-finder, you will find new innovative ways to be successful and drive your career to new heights.

Most successful business owners got where they are because they were innovative.

ISLAND LORE

We created an imaginary island. Was that innovative? Thomas Edison would probably say, "Not really ... but at least you're trying." Thanks, Tommy (blush)

Not everybody will innovate like Steve Jobs, but it shouldn't dissuade us from trying.

At the very least, you are moving mental muscles that sit dormant in most humans.

Rule No. 134

ANALYZE THIS

As a salesperson, you have no shortage of things to analyze.

Analyze your territory and how to grow your business.

Analyze the metrics, your sales goals, your process, your pipeline, your closing percentages, your conversion rates and more …

Analyze, analyze, analyze, because numbers never lie.

In the same breath, can we tell you not to overanalyze?

We won't get into how over-analyzing can kill you, because that message would be too confusing.

Analyze—but not too much.

ISLAND LORE

Don't be a victim of paralysis by analysis.

Rule 136
CHARACTER MATTERS

People who've been successful in business for any length of time didn't get there by putting their faith in just anyone. They are very careful about who they trust.

So how do you, as a salesperson, earn this trust? Well, you can develop it over an extended period of time, proving to the client that you are worthy.

ISLAND LORE

The Island is full of character—and characters.

But it's much easier, and faster, to come into the business relationship with an already-impeccable reputation. If you are known for your outstanding character and trustworthiness, you're that much closer to a sale.

Break the mold. Be the person people trust.

Rule 137

ALWAYS DO YOUR RESEARCH

Elite salespeople always do their homework. They are thoroughly prepared—without fail.

Whatever you need know about your sale, research it. Turn over every last stone until you're fully prepared.

Going into a sales meeting unprepared is the kiss of death.

Enough said. We hope.

ISLAND LORE

If you're unprepared, the client will eat you up faster than the sharks that patrol the Island's coast, waiting for the "unprepareds" to wander out beyond the sand bar.

Rule 138

STUDY LANGUAGE

If you've ever met a politician, you know what this tip is all about.

The words we use are crucial in determining an outcome.

Your speech can always improve, and there's no shortage of great literature out there on language to use when influencing others.

But, unless you're the President of the United States and have an entire staff working on your speeches, you're going to have to learn effective language on your own.

ISLAND LORE

We know, never talk politics. But it's true: Politicians are masters of speech. (At least, the good ones are.)

There is a science behind the language you use.

Which of these following sentences sounds better?
• Just sign on the dotted line.
• Would you care to read over the agreement?

Rule 139
NETWORK

Asking for referrals is one of the smartest ways to make money, and just one example of how to network.

Like with anything else in life, who you know can be more important than what you know.

Invest in people.

The more information you have, the more people you know, the more valuable you are.

A strong network is priceless.

This is another rule that applies to life as well as sales.

ISLAND LORE

You are now part of what will be the largest sales network ever! Just watch!

Rule 140
DISCOVER PAIN POINTS

Try your best to determine what the pain is that your prospect is experiencing and how your product or service can solve that problem.

Once you have determined what your prospect's pain is, incorporate your solutions into the rest of your conversation.

This technique will constantly remind your client what life without pain will be like.

ISLAND LORE

On the Island, your pain will be eased with a healthy dose of bonfires, great tunes, and stimulating conversations. Paradise … we know.

Rule No. 140

Rule 141
BE INDIFFERENT

Indifference is defined as the lack of emotion, motivation or enthusiasm.

Sounds pretty bad, right? But in fact, indifference is a powerful tool when used in the right situations.

Sometimes, when you're closing a deal, it's important to convey a certain amount of indifference.

Your only concern is that they get what they need.

If a customer senses that you covet the sale too much, it's a guaranteed turn off.

ISLAND LORE

If your customer doesn't buy your product or service, it's their life that is affected the most.

If you truly want what is best for the client, you will convey the perfect amount of indifference.

Rule 142

THINK BIG

You can get whatever you want, but it all starts with your mindset.

If you think big, you will talk big. And then your results will be big!

ISLAND LORE #1

Maybe we should have named it the Nation of Sales, or the Planet of Sales ... or even the Galaxy of Sales.

ISLAND LORE #2

We needed to add an additional Island Lore here, because ironically, the rule which we titled "Think BIG" was far too SMALL ... but you get the point.

Rule 143

CONTROL, CONTROL, CONTROL

It's obviously a good idea to always remain in control of your prospects and the sales process.

Outlining your agenda from the outset of the sales process helps you gain immediate control.

If you have a clear path of what you want to do and you announce this to your customer, it's much easier to control the call. Buyers want to be led.

And remember: You can have control and still be extremely courteous.

If your customer truly wants your product or service, they will be happy to be in the hands of an authoritative salesperson who is controlling the conversation.

In more than 65% of all sales calls made in the U.S. today, the salesperson will never ask for the order, but instead wait for the prospect to "buy".

Rule 144

TAKE OWNERSHIP IN YOUR COMPANY

This book is meant for sales professionals of all stripes.

Regardless of your title or position—C-level executive or entry-level associate who only recently arrived on the Island—you have to take ownership in the company you work for.

Act as if you're the majority shareholder in the company, and make decisions accordingly.

> ## ISLAND LORE
>
> While we encourage you to act like you own the company, we don't recommend taking your boss's parking space!

Pretend that you own the company. Each day, match the work ethic of the hardest working person in the company. Carry yourself like the most important person in the company and someday you just might be.

Rule 145
ADAPT TO EVERYTHING

What happens to a species that fails to adapt to changes in its environment?

Yup. It becomes extinct.

If you're reading this book, we're guessing "career extinction" isn't high on your list of goals. If you want to survive—and thrive—in sales, you have to be able to adapt to anything and everything that comes your way.

ISLAND LORE

Salespeople should adapt to every environment by melting right into the landscape—like a chameleon. (Just don't start singing Boy George songs!)

Tone. Pace. Intellect. Cultural differences. Jet lag. Language (formal or informal). Cadence. Eye contact. Body language. Bad hair day. Personalities. Humor. Office environment. Competition. Economic shifts. An insane boss ... the list is endless.

Adapt and prosper.

Rule No. 145

Rule 146

BE BOLD AND COURAGEOUS

Boldness is an interesting characteristic. Too much is bad, while too little is … well … too little.

At this point in your life, you should know how bold you are. If it's your nature to be bold and brash, to the point of obnoxiousness, try dialing it down a few notches when it comes to sales. Practice a little caution and "humble" boldness.

If, on the other hand, it's your nature to be timid and meek, start asserting yourself more in your career. Bold people get things done. Don't be afraid to stand up for what you believe in or to take risks.

ISLAND LORE

As writers, we'll never be confused with Hemingway or Twain. But we still wrote a book. Bold? You bet your ass! Almost as bold as saying, "You bet your ass" in a business book!

We're not saying you have to go boldly where no man has gone before. But you can still go … carefully.

Rule No. 146

Island of Sales

Rule 147

AVOID CAUSING DECISION PARALYSIS

We were going to mention on the cover of this book how you can fan its pages in front of your face on a hot summer's day to cool off. Or, how in a pinch you can use the inside cover to jot down a telephone number or even how nice it might look on your coffee table, right next to your coffee table book about coffee tables …

… But our marketing department decided to just focus on the fact that it's a Pocket Guide for Sales Survival.

When you give your prospects too much information, it can easily cloud the picture, muddle the sales cycle, and, ultimately, lead to rejection.

> ## ISLAND LORE
>
> If you're looking for a coffee table, our book does not turn into a coffee table; See Cosmo for that.

If your customer needs the product to roll and swing, talk to them about how great it rolls and swings. Don't overwhelm them with the fact that it jumps, skips, wiggles and climbs. They only need it to roll and swing.

Overselling can cause decision paralysis. It's great that your product has dozens of features, but the prospect might think that it's more than they need and head to a product that only rolls and swings.

Rule No. 147

Rule 148

ACQUIRE QUALITY CUSTOMERS

Quantity is nice, but nothing beats quality.

It's much easier to upsell a current customer than it is to get a brand new one.

The right customers are the ones who will re-buy, renew, and reinvest. Acquire quality customers.

The quickest route to the "Sales Hall of Shame" is high attrition.

If your deals always cancel, something is wrong, Amigo.

ISLAND LORE

Get sales as often as you can while you're on the Island, but make sure to also bring the right customers aboard.

Rule 149
HAVE UNIQUE EXPERIENCES

Sales can get pretty repetitive. For many of us, we sell the same product or service for years.

If that's the case, it means you're using the same sales pitch thousands of times! You're repeating the same information day in and day out, week after week, month after month, year after year, decade after ... OK.

The point is that it's easy to get complacent.

ISLAND LORE

Is there even such a thing as an cappuccino espresso latte? If there isn't, we'll invent it just for the Island. Take that, Starbucks!

Never let the repetition show.

Every new prospect deserves a unique, top-notch experience with you. Don't ever cheat your customers out of an exhilarating, informative presentation. Stay on your game.

Your sales pitch at 4:45 on a Friday afternoon should sound exactly like the first pitch you threw out on Monday morning—after your first cappuccino espresso latte.

Rule No. 149

Rule 150
BE A SERVANT LEADER

A servant leader is someone who is servant first and everything else second.

Have a desire to help others on your team and contribute to the well-being of your customers.

A servant leader looks to the needs of the people and always looks into how they can help their people solve problems and promote personal development.

> ## ISLAND LORE
>
> Here on the Island, we are your humble servants. Would you like a fresh towel? Perhaps another mudslide?

When you act as a servant in sales, you place your main focus on people and helping them get what they need.

This in turn will lead to more sales for you and yours.

Rule 151

TALK ABOUT THE FUTURE

Every customer wants to know what their business (or life) will be like once they have purchased your product or solution.

Educate customers about how your product or service will impact their lives.

For the customers with people-oriented personalities, use testimonials.

ISLAND LORE

Heavy stuff, huh? There is that word again …"heavy." Why is everything so heavy on the Island? Is there a problem with the Earth's gravitational pull?

For the customers with task-oriented personalities, use lists.

Either way, you will be giving them a vision of happiness.

Labor statistics show that the USA is expected to create two million new sales jobs by 2020, increasing the demand for professional salespeople immensly!

Rule 152

EVERYONE IS A WHALE

Never discriminate against small prospects or large ones.

We all love to land that whale, but if you treat everyone as if they will someday be a whale; your boat will soon be overflowing with prize catches.

It's truly impossible to know what a customer will bring in the future. They may only buy one now, but they may come back for 20—and bring all their friends with them.

Beyond that, it's just the right thing to do. Everyone is a whale!

ISLAND LORE

On the Island, there are whale watches every day at 4 p.m. Don't worry—we get you back in time for happy hour!

TELL PEOPLE WHAT TO DO

Telling your prospect what to do will work more often than you may think.

Picture yourself brushing your teeth.

Now, picture yourself in a toga brushing your teeth.

See? People will do what you tell them to do.

Pretty simple.

Don't be afraid to (nicely) tell your prospects what to do, because when it comes down to it, they probably will.

ISLAND LORE

Can you please do something for us? Go tell all your friends, relatives and colleagues to buy this book. Thanks! Sorry, we can't help it ... what do you expect? Oh yes, the website! Here it is: www.thebestsalesbook.com

Rule 154

VERIFY NEEDS AND VERIFY SOLUTIONS

Never forget the power of repeating what a prospect has said. When prospects identify what their needs are, verify them by repeating them out loud.

Prospect – "I spend so much time trying to find relevant content for my blog and Twitter, there just isn't enough time in the day."

You – "Ok, so you need an efficiency tool that can save you time and update your blog and social media regularly with new, fresh content consistently? Ok, no problem, I have the perfect tool for that. www.curata.com"

It is important that your prospect knows that you were listening and the there is a reason you have suggested this particular solution.

ISLAND LORE

If you were sick, wouldn't you like to know what you have and what the medication is supposed to do? Imagine going to the doctor and being told that you are "sick" and need to "take this medicine." Wait. What? Why? How? When?

It's not rocket science, it's people science.

ACKNOWLEDGE OTHER PEOPLE'S SUCCESS

As a true salesperson, you are extremely competitive and you want to be the best at all costs.

If and when the chips don't fall in your corner, acknowledge the success of others.

It could be your superior, a direct report or a peer. Spread the congratulations no matter where they sit in the organizational flowchart.

ISLAND LORE

We want success for others. We know we will get ours, so we are truly happy for you when you succeed.

Learn how to bury your competitiveness when you have lost, reach down deep, find true selflessness, and let it out.

Rule 156

APPEAL TO EMOTION & LOGIC

People expect a logical solution. Just be prepared for them to become emotional about the solution!

Remember this key theory: Emotion drives your customer's impulse, but logic will always be their guide.

Pay attention and appeal to both of these elements, and you will have more success.

ISLAND LORE

It's a fact that people spend money to ease pain. Case in point: How many times have you purchased aspirin to cure a headache? We rest our case ... and our aching heads.

Get your prospects talking about how they feel—get them to express emotion—and then close.

It's only logical.

BE CONFIDENT – YOU ARE THE EXPERT

Can you imagine Vince Lombardi getting up before his team and fumbling around with notes, not sure what to say before a game?

Can you picture Steven Spielberg leaving his cast and crew twiddling their thumbs on the set while he second- and third-guesses himself, struggling to make a simple decision?

ISLAND LORE

If you're constantly saying, "I have to ask my boss," maybe you should have your boss sell for you, too.

Can you imagine the President of the United States stuttering and stammering, unable to get his point across during his State of the Union address?

You are the expert, and everyone is counting on you to be confident.

Carry yourself with confidence. You are the expert. Act like it.

Rule 158

USE A CONSULTATIVE APPROACH

Most salespeople fear being too pushy or too aggressive. There is one way to never come off pushy, and that is to always act as a consultant. If you uncover specific needs and truly care about meeting those needs, you will never come off pushy.

This approach is a mental challenge for all salespeople. It dictates that you must focus on caring about the customer instead of yourself. If you're thinking about your sales goal and how you "need this sale" to hit your goal, you will not be a consultant.

Picture yourself walking with your arm around a customer's shoulder. Your tone changes when you put your arm around someone. Or picture yourself sitting on the same side of a table as a customer, instead of on the opposite side. Your tone and inflection changes in both of these situations.

ISLAND LORE

Always talk with people, not at people. Educate your customers, don't "sell" them. On the Island we only want what is best for you. Period.

Rule No. 158

Rule 159

INVESTIGATE BY ASKING STRATEGIC QUESTIONS

Selling is NOT about forcing someone to purchase something they do not need. Selling is actually about listening to your customer's needs to determine whether your product is a good fit.

Most of the time they will tell you exactly what they are looking for. It's more about listening and uncovering all of the pain points or needs.

Always prepare a half dozen questions that are not only strategic, but also open-ended.

Always start sentences with the phrase "Tell me about" or "Help me understand." These are perfect ways to begin an open-ended question.

ISLAND LORE

Try these on your next call: Tell me more about your timeline … or … Help me understand the budget you are working with … or … Would you mind sharing with me what you are currently looking for …

The questions you ask will give you the information you need to close the deal.

Rule 160
ANCHOR HIGH

A real anchor falls down to the ocean floor easier than it comes back up to the boat.

So when you mention price, you must anchor high and come down if needed. Not the other way around.

If the first price you mention is the lowest price available, good luck trying to sell someone something more expensive.

It is simple psychology that people would rather save money than spend more. When presenting your product and price you have three choices.

Give the exact price it will cost
Mention a higher price, then lower it
Mention the lowest price, then raise it

We suggest either option 1 or 2.

ISLAND LORE

Let gravity pull your anchor down to the lowest price possible. If you are smart, you'll end up landing halfway between the surface and the mud.

Rule 161

THE DIFFERENCE

How much does the winning horse typically win by in the
Kentucky Derby?"

A nose.

When a swimmer wins the Olympics or a runner wins the 100 meter
dash, how much do they win by?

A couple hundredths of a second.

The difference between good and great ... is not that much. If you
consistently do just a little bit more, you will consistently be just a little
bit better.

Go into work tomorrow a few minutes early or stay at work tonight a
few minutes late.

Stop to tell a coworker what a great job they are doing, ask a coworker
how their significant other or family are doing, tidy up the office, call a
customer and ask how things are going ... all very simple, little things
that ANYONE can do.

Becoming successful is typically not defined by one single event, it is the
combination of thousands of tiny events that add up over time. Maybe
that horse who wins the Kentucky Derby each year spends just 15
minutes more per day in training than the other horses.

Maybe the Gold medalists in the Olympics do 3 more pushups a day than silver and bronze ... and maybe, just maybe, you will be number 1 in the next 5 years by getting into work just 30 minutes earlier each day.

You only have to sell one dollar more that the number 2 person in your company to be number 1.

Ask yourself what you can do tomorrow to be just a little bit better than today.

Growth and success are not about perfection, they are about progression. Consistently growing and getting better until you are the best.

So decide to do just a little bit more.

You might be surprised to find that you are just a little bit better.

ISLAND LORE

Can you imagine a company full of salespeople who do just a little bit more?

Rule No. 161

THE CLOSE
By Randy Bernard

I'm encouraged, and I'll tell you why.

I didn't realize it then, but over a decade ago I officially arrived on The Island of Sales. I started my first real sales job.

And it was brutal.

The job was outside sales, going from house to house or business to business. (Wherever they dropped you off). The job consisted of simply knocking on doors all day long and trying to sell people stuff.

If you didn't knock on at least 100 doors on a given day, you simply weren't working hard enough. To make matters worse, I was working on 100% commission. No base pay, no hourly wage, no benefits and absolutely no end in sight.

And yet, this job was the best thing that ever happened to me.

It was, without question, the most rigorous and thorough sales training one could ask for, but I didn't know that at the time.

I could share horror stories with you for days about being broke, stranded, yelled at, spit on, and having things thrown at me. I have true stories about being bitten by dogs, physically thrown out of office buildings, not making sales for days and vivid memories about times when I knew that the only way I was going to eat my next meal was if I closed a sale.

I can tell you about how many times I wanted to quit, how many times my friends and family TOLD me to quit, and even about the times when my friends nearly scheduled an intervention to FORCE me to quit.

I can give you 1,000 reasons why I shouldn't be here today, writing this book, completely immersed in a sales career almost 15 years later. But instead, I will tell you why I am here.

And I owe it ALL to discouragement. That's right, discouragement.

People spend a lot of time trying to pinpoint the precise moment when they fell in love with their significant other, or when they determined which career was right for them.

I know exactly why I'm fortunate enough to have survived one of the toughest careers in the world, a sales career. I can trace it all back to a single moment in time. I remember it perfectly.

It was 8:30 a.m. on Jan. 6, 2000. I was in Burbank, California, at a small sales company on Olive Avenue. The owner, Jaime Hepp, was conducting our morning meeting. It was my very first week on the job and, more importantly, it was one week away from my arrival on The Island of Sales.

It was one of those morning meetings where someone stands up and tries to fire everyone up with enough motivation to get us through another grueling day of 100 doors—95 of which would certainly be slamming in our faces.

Jaime stood up in front of the room full of two dozen eager, impressionable, rookie salespeople ready for their daily injection of wisdom. He told us a story about the Devil's yard sale, originally written by William Roedel Rathvon. It went something like this:

One day, the Devil decided he was going to go out of business and sell all of his tools. They were attractively displayed on tables in his yard with price tags hanging from each. On the tables were malice, greed, envy, hate, jealousy, dishonesty and more.

The Close

A passerby looked at all of the items for sale, noticed something strange and decided to ask the Devil about what he saw.

"Devil?" he said. "You have many different tools for sale here, and all of them look like beautiful, shiny, elegant items that you use in your trade. But I couldn't help but notice that dirty, old, rusty wedge-shaped tool on the rear table. It's priced much higher than the rest. What is it?"

"That is discouragement," the Devil said. "The reason that item is priced so much higher than all the rest is because it is with that item, and that item ONLY, that I can pry open a person's consciousness, and only then allow all of my other tools inside to do their work. Without discouragement, I couldn't even get close with the others."

I remember all too well the feeling I used to get in my stomach when the owner, Jaime, would start wrapping up his morning meetings. Every day, as his stories drew to a close, waves of fear, embarrassment and nervousness would wash over my entire body. These feelings sat heavy in my gut because I knew that as soon as he made his point and finished his meeting, it would be time for us to head out into the unknown for another day of complete cold-calling hell. Sometimes I wished his stories would go on for hours. But not this day.

This is the moment that changed my life. This is the moment that allowed me to have the success that I've been so fortunate to enjoy. That story is the single most important reason why I'm still here today.

Why? Well, had I heard that story a year later, a month later or maybe even a week later, it would have been too late. I would have quit a long time ago. Maybe I would have quit on the first day that I failed to make a single dollar. Maybe I would have quit when I was bit by that dog or thrown out of that building. Regardless of when, I would have quit.

The day I heard that story, I understood one of the most crucial necessities of being a sales professional. I learned to focus on the one thing I CAN control: my attitude.

More specifically, I learned how to manage discouragement.

It was simple. It made so much sense.

Don't get discouraged! No matter what.

Regardless of what happens, don't let that "tool" get inside your consciousness, or else …

I've gone on to face plenty of obstacles in the 15 years since I heard that story. I've had tough times, challenges and failures, but all the while I remembered the moral of the story.

We've all been discouraged from time to time, and it's only then that we think about quitting. It's only then that we consider taking shortcuts. Discouragement causes anger, fear, resentment, and, ultimately, weakness and failure.

As you finish this book, I IMPLORE you to do two things starting immediately.

First, you must train yourself to consciously recognize the exact moment when you are feeling the slightest bit of discouragement. You will feel it coming on, just as you do when you are tired, hungry, or lonely.

To survive on The Island of Sales, you must recognize discouragement the moment it rears its ugly head.

Second, you must do everything in your power to rid your mind and cleanse your body of those feelings of discouragement. If you can, everything else will take care of itself.

I started off by saying that I am encouraged, and this is why: I am encouraged for you.

I was fortunate to have an amazing mentor, Jaime Hepp, to guide

The Close

me through those challenges. I will not tell you that I've never been discouraged since that day—I certainly have—but I have been able to squash that discouragement quickly as an act of self-preservation.

Jason and I can't walk the streets with you tomorrow and tell you to keep your chin up after that first prospect says "no." I can't sit at your desk with you next week and encourage you after you lose a sale and feel like giving up. Jason can't be with you in your car or on the train, reminding you of crucial sales rules as a deal hangs in the balance.

We can't be there with you, but this book can.

That's why I feel encouraged.

You may not have known it, may not have asked for it, and may not have realized it until now, but you live on The Island of Sales with us, and you have no choice but to survive.

This book is not meant to motivate you; it is meant to assist you, guide you, and help you survive.

I am encouraged because you now have the essentials. You have the story. You can use this book on a daily basis and remind yourself about the crucial cornerstones necessary to survive on the Island. I am encouraged because if you read this book and share it with others, you will conquer discouragement.

I am encouraged because you now know where to draw the strength to fight off discouragement.

To all of my fellow salespeople, I empathize with your obstacles, but always remember:

The strength lies within The Island of Sales. That strength is your ability to help others.

Keep this pocket guide nearby as a token of strength. Share these lessons so together we can thrive on The Island of Sales.

These are the essentials. This is our Guide for Survival.

-Randy Bernard

Thank you for reading the essentials...

This is your Pocket Guide For Sales Survival.

THANK YOU

The Editors

Ed Brennen
Thank you to Ed Brennen. Ed you took on this project and attacked it. You gave this book flow, humor, and expression. Your contribution to this book is monumental. Thank you for everything you did. You are one talented and fun person to work with.

Bethany Parker
Thank you Bethany for taking this project on at a hectic time in your life. Your editing and proofing was critical to the flow and accuracy of this book. You are a very gifted writer that we are lucky to work with.

Ariane Mandell
Thank you for proofing this book and your amazing words of encouragement. Your attention to detail was outstanding and also reminded us to sign up for grammar classes. You are such a talented person on so many levels, we are so lucky to have you on our team.

The Design Team

Nate Cameron, Adam Schwartz, Jeff Vogel and Christian Gilbert. We are so greatful you guys came into the picture and gave this book its new bold look. Your creative and logical compass was exactly what we needed. Your talent and quick turnaround time was amazing. This version 2.0 was all you guys! Thank you!

JASON'S GRATITUDE

Thank you to all the amazing people who have contributed love, wisdom and support.

Ella and Eva
You are the greatest gifts I will ever experience. I hope someday you understand how deep my love for you is. I hope you then know why you are first. Always and forever, you are first. Thank you for inspiring everything I do. You give me the gift of feeling like the luckiest man in the world. Sunflowers and tulips.

My family
Mom, Dad, Janelle, Brian, Jeff, Merette, Lynley, Sue, Ella, Eva, George, Gerri, Dave. All of you have provided support and love at different times and in different ways. Words cannot express my gratitude.

And to everyone else
There are too many people to name. I tried to list everyone and it was impossible. I try to glean information and inspiration from everyone I know. If you have been there, you know who you are. You all at some point have been there to listen, offer advice and most importantly, care. I have so much respect and gratitude for all of you.

Jason's Gratitude

RANDY'S GRATITUDE

I would like to thank my wife Jamie-Lynn, for her infinite trust and support and for making me laugh every single day. Huge thanks to my Mom and Dad for always leading by example and teaching me how to be a man of my word and a generous, compassionate friend. Thank you to my kids, Gage and Logan, for inspiring me to always do my best.

Jaime Hepp – My first mentor
The best decision I made for my career was trusting in you. Your coaching and guidance early in my professional life gave me the dedication and desire to strive for my goals and the resilience to hit them.

To:
Joe Matekel, Joe Nolan, Cory Riffer, Mike Rivera, Jeff Gomez, Beth Lovernick, Luke St. Germaine, Scott Williams, Justin Jordan, Christina Englehardt, Sean Vernon, Maria Villena, Mehdi Kouchtaf, Steve Cardenas, James Dobbs, and everyone else that worked with me in California ...

You all motivate me, simple as that. I never got an opportunity to truly repay you for your unwavering faith in me, your undeniable trust, and years of hard work, but not a day goes by that I don't wish that I could make you all millionaires. Thank you for believing in me, I love you all.

ACKNOWLEDGEMENTS

We could not and probably would not have written this book without inspiration from these authors and their and inspiring and educational books.

How to Win Friends and Influence People – Dale Carnegie
The 21 Irrefutable Laws of Leadership – John Maxwell
Today Matters – John Maxwell
Fish – Stephen C. Lundin, Harry Paul, John Christensen
Switch – Chip Heath and Dan Heath
Good to Great – Jim Collins
Linchpin – Seth Godin
Socialnomics –Erik Qualman
The Alchemist – Paulo Coelho
The 7 Habits of Highly Effective People – Stephen R. Covey
The Greatest Salesman in the World – Og Mandino

The Sales University Movement
We must also acknowledge the amazing work being done by the Sales Education Foundation to promote sales programs at Universities all over the world. Please visit their website: www.saleseducationfoundation.org

Please pay specific attention to the Universities who already offer sales programs and are always looking for support.

www.saleseducationfoundation.org/html/univ-list

We cannot stress how much we believe in this movement and will always support it the best we can. We feel students studying sales in college is a complete game changer for the global economy.

Acknowledgements

Special thanks to these Universities who are running some of the top rated sales programs in the world:

Elon University –Dr. Michael Rodriguez

The College of New Jersey – Dr. Al Pelham

University of Connecticut – Bill Ryan

Florida State University – Pat Pallentino

The following companies are sales recruiting firms that we use to find great sales candidates. If you are a sales person looking for a career change, or a company looking for talented salespeople, contact these companies:

Salestart – www.salestartnow.com

Dana Associates – www.danaassociates.com

Rubenstein Careers – hrubenstein@verizon.net

J.David Group – webb@thejdavidgroup.com

HireMinds LLC – scott@hireminds.com

This is a list of great companies to work at:

EF Education First – www.ef.com

Curata – www.curata.com

Hubspot – www.hubspot.com

Yodle – www.yodle.com

Oracle – www.oracle.com

Google – www.google.com

Facebook – www.facebook.com

Salestart – www.salestartnow.com

Salesforce – www.salesforce.com

Goldman Sachs – www.goldmansachs.com

Millennium: The Takeda Oncology Company – www.mlnm.com

The Boston Consulting Group – www.bcg.com

Ernst & Young – www.ey.com

Zappos – www.zappos.com

Apple – www.apple.com

Sandler Training – www.sandler.com

Thank You

Special thanks to the people who chipped in with specific insight for this book. Even though we may not have used everything that was submitted, we are very grateful for your help:
Brandon Walters Gullicksen (brandonsboards.com),
Chris Bernard, Jim Secondiani, Dean Soulia, Scott Infantolino, Doreen Perley, Joe Matekel, Will Cronin, James Dobbs, Vera Quinn, Jaime Hepp, David Horowitz, Ryan Hensley, Casey Gallagher, Joe Nolan, Joe Harvey, Brandi Longtin, Ted Ciolkosz, Brian Pinkham

Sales websites facts and figures
www.salestalent.com/Selling-Facts.html
www.saleseducationfoundation.org
www.bizcommunity.com
www.insidesales.com
www.buzzbuilderpro.com
hbr.org

Thank you

INDEX

Stories

Rules

Index

Index

Index

IF YOU ENJOYED THE POCKET GUIDE FOR SALES SURVIVAL

Please suggest it to others at

www.thebestsalesbook.com

Fin

NOTES FOR SALES SURVIVAL